The Senior's Guide to Dog Ownership

The Senior's Guide to Dog Ownership:
How to Love, Care for and Keep Your Best Friend

Myrna L. Papurt, B.Sc, DVM

Croce Publishing, LLC

Leonia, New Jersey

With special acknowledgement to the late Richard W. Redding, DVM, M.Sc., Ph.D. His ideas and encouragement were instrumental in the writing of this book.

Published in 2008 by Croce Publishing, LLC
PO Box 449
Leonia, NJ 07605
Web site: http://www.crocepublishing.com
Email: info@crocepublishing.com

Library of Congress Cataloging-in-Publication Data

Papurt, M. L. (Myrna L.)
The senior's guide to dog ownership : how to love, care for and keep your best friend / Myrna L. Papurt.
p. cm.
Includes index.
ISBN 978-0-9719538-5-7 (alk. paper)
1. Dogs. I. Title.

SF427.P216 2008
636.7'0887--dc22

2008002667

Printed in the United States of America

CONTENTS

Introduction
Another Heartbeat in the House

The voice on the phone was crying so hard that I could not understand her words. The speaker struggled to compose herself. Finally she gasped "Doctor, do you think you could find a home for Sunny?"

I realized that the speaker was Arlene Hudson, the owner of a ten-year-old yellow Labrador retriever. Arlene was a widow, an older lady, devoted to her pet, and Sunny was a really nice dog—why would she give him up?

When I asked this question, Arlene started to cry again. "I'm going to have surgery and the doctor says I can't keep him. You know how he pulls on the leash. The doctor says I mustn't be jerked around. But without Sunny, I'll be all alone."

I was startled. Sunny was Arlene's entire life. "There must be something else you could do. I know how you love him."

"I'd do anything to keep him...anything. But the doctor says."

Arlene Hudson was the victim of a problem common to many seniors. You may find that you are no longer able to deal with some of the behaviors of your cherished canine companion. Or you may be forced by circumstances to change your mode of living. Perhaps you have physical limitations that prevent you from coping with your dogs' needs and activities. Your family or your doctor propose a "simple" solution: get rid of the dog.

But is this solution so simple? You love your dog. You may have had animals most of your life and you would feel totally lost without your pet. Your heart cries out "I want to keep my dog. There must be a way."

Arlene was still sobbing over the phone. "Stop crying, Arlene," I said, "let's figure this out. Just exactly why do you think you have to give up the dog?"

"Well, the doctor insists that I can't be jumped on or yanked around."

"Does Sunny jump on you?

"Just when I first come home, but…."

"Does he yank you around?"

"Only when I take him out on a leash. He has a choke collar, too."

"Anything else?" By this time, I was very disturbed. I knew that giving up her dog would be a great blow to Arlene.

"No, his pulling and jumping are the main problems. But my daughter said that at least I wouldn't have all that yellow hair to sweep up. You know how Sunny sheds."

Yes, I thought. All dogs shed. But shedding is not a crime punishable by shattering two lives. It was beginning to sound as though neither her doctor nor her daughter were aware, as I was, of the strength of this owner and this dog's emotional bond and the consequences to Arlene of tearing it apart.

"Arlene," I said. "I know how much you want to keep Sunny. The problems you mentioned are really pretty simple. Let's figure out some solutions."

We discussed the many and varied methods and devices that enable a relatively weak owner to have physical control over an energetic dog. We arranged for Arlene and Sunny to try several types of anti-pull collars and leads, and to select the most effective one for her. I described to Arlene how to get Sunny to replace his jumping-up with "sit-stay." Once Sunny learned to sit and stay with all four feet on the ground, he never again jumped up on Arlene. Arlene was ecstatic. "Maybe I can convince my doctor and my daughter to let me keep Sunny."

"You don't have to convince anyone to allow you to keep your dog," I told Arlene. "Of course you should listen to your doctor's advice, but you are a responsible adult. You can make your own decisions. There are ways to solve your problems that will let you keep Sunny.

What are the reasons to keep my dog?

Thirty-five million Americans are over 65 years of age. Many have lost some or all of our closest associates; spouses die, children become adults and have their own lives, friends no longer call. Without their dogs, a significant number of senior citizens would live alone. Many would experience increased loneliness, inactivity and fear.

Health professionals say that both the physical health and the mental health of senior citizens are enhanced by their beloved dogs. The American Medical Association, the American Veterinary Medical Association, the American Society for the Prevention of Cruelty to Animals, the Delta Society: Health Benefits of Animals, physicians that specialize in geriatrics and many other organizations attest to this. Everybody tells us to keep our dogs. Nobody tells us how to do it.

You never will be alone.

Companionship, of course, is why we have dogs. Dogs give

us something to care for, something to talk to, something to welcome us home. The silence of an empty house is not absolute whenever there is the presence of another living thing.

You will keep more active.

It's difficult, in fact probably impossible, to be sedentary with a dog around. Dogs have to be cared for; dogs have to be let out and let back in, dogs need to be walked and exercised, fed and brushed. The physical activity associated with dog ownership has been shown to be of great benefit to seniors' cardiovascular function, muscle tone, bone strength, respiration, even their immune systems. Seniors who have dogs are much more likely to engage in walking and other exercise than those that are alone.

You will have an early warning system.

As we age, our senses of hearing and sight diminish. Whether we live alone or with others, we can feel insecure in today's increasingly hostile world. Especially in urban areas, we seniors are in the age group most likely to be victimized by intruders in our homes or in our cars. Even if our dog is not a huge pit bull, its barking lets a thief or molester know that we know he's there and we have called for help.

Years ago, the protective value of even a small dog was demonstrated to me very clearly. One of my clients was an elderly man who lived in a motor home with his 20-pound Welsh terrier. Taffy was perfectly friendly with whomever the owner invited in, but she behaved like a 20-pound piranha if a stranger dared to approach within a few feet of the vehicle. The owner bragged that he never had a single fear about the danger of intruders, night or day.

Many dog problems have simple solutions.

Physical limitations and handicaps often affect our ability to care for our dog. Special techniques and methods are necessary to help us if we use a cane or a walker, or are confined to wheelchairs. If we have diminished eyesight or hearing, we need other techniques to minimize our problem. But there are ways—many ways—to handle each of our problems and to allow us to keep and enjoy our dogs.

Dog ownership is not without expense. Dogs must be fed, dogs must receive veterinary care, and there are times when dogs must be boarded or be professionally groomed. You must know which dog-related expenses are absolutely necessary and which are extras. You need to know what kinds of foods are convenient and nutritionally complete and which are unnecessarily expensive and messy. If you are on a limited income, you should not have to choose between buying dog food and buying your own medications.

Pet-friendly rentals may be hard to find. If you don't own your own home or if you find it necessary to move to smaller rental quarters, you may be faced with a dilemma. Many rental properties specify "no pets," and with good reason: renters are notorious for being careless about pet damage.

Some landlords can be persuaded to accept a deposit to be held against possible damage. Some can be convinced of the good behavior of the dog and the commitment to damage control of the senior owner.

You might move in with members of your family. Families may have their own dogs; they may not welcome another dog; they may not want dogs at all. These problems must be worked out on an individual basis, but solutions usually exist that can make it possible to take your dog with you to a new home.

You might want to travel. In some instances, the dog can travel, too. By automobile or by plane, there are procedures to be followed that allow seniors to be accompanied by their pets.

When the dog absolutely must be left behind, friends, family, or boarding kennels can be used to keep the dog safe and comfortable in your absence. Guidelines can help you decide what arrangements are best.

At the end: what will happen if your dog becomes terminally ill or severely incapacitated? You must know how to handle the situation humanely and wisely And what will happen to your cherished companion if it outlives you? Who will care for it and value it as you did? With a little information, you can determine what will happen to your dog if you die first, and you can make binding legal arrangements for your wishes to be carried out.

There are better solutions than "get rid of that dog." There are methods, equipment and techniques that will enable you to solve your dog problems. Let's utilize all the resources at our disposal and keep our best friend.

Part I: Controlling Your Dog's Behavior

Chapter 1
<u>When Your Dog is Unruly in the House</u>

❝Mom, that dog is going to knock you down and hurt you.

Besides, it's making a wreck of the house and the neighbors are complaining about the noise. Why don't you let me take it to the pound?"

Everyone would like to own a nice quiet dog that does what it's told. Unfortunately, many of our dogs don't quite fit that description. Quite a lot of dogs jump on people, get on furniture, bark at everything, chew up things, sneak out the door whenever they can, and generally disregard the word "no." As we become seniors, we are less willing or able to cope with behaviors that younger people merely find annoying.

What are the choices: Live with the undesirable behavior, part with the dog or control the behavior? Since living with unruly behavior is often impossible and parting with the dog is a very sad option, we must find out how to control our dogs' transgressions.

"But I couldn't punish my dog." Nobody likes the word punish because it implies inflicting pain. Humane dog training is a blend of favorable stimuli (food and praise) and adverse stimuli (things the dog doesn't like or tries to avoid) but should never include inflicting pain.

It is much more humane to correct your dog's bad habits than to relinquish it to an uncertain future. There are many ways to solve our problems.

How do I keep Rover from jumping on me?

When your dog jumps on you, it can do a lot of harm. You may get scratched, dirty, or have your clothes torn. Much worse, you may be knocked down and injured. If your dog jumps on an unsuspecting guest or stranger, you might even have a lawsuit.

Your dog will jump on you most often when it is greeting you, such as when you come home. This is a natural attention-seeking behavior; the dog is happy to see you and wants to get as close as possible. Dogs also jump on you when you are eating or holding an attractive-looking object.

Most methods advocated to stop your dog from jumping on you are not very successful. Raising a knee to knock the dog backward or stepping on its back paws is difficult enough for agile people; it is likely to be impossible if you need to keep both feet firmly on the ground.

Some trainers will tell you to turn away from the dog so that the side of your body is toward the dog. Some tell you to step backward so the dog cannot get its feet on you. Most jumping dogs are quick to make adjustments to these maneuvers and jump on you anyway. Train your dog to do something else instead of jumping.

Training Rover to sit.

Your dog probably already knows the command to sit. In case it doesn't, this is the easiest command in the dog's repertoire; every training book tells you how to teach sit. Hold a treat above the dog's head while saying "sit." Move the treat backward so the dog will sit to look up at the food. Give the dog the treat when it sits. Very soon the dog will associate sitting with getting a nice little morsel.

If your dog doesn't sit automatically to look up at the treat, you'll have to push its hindquarters down with your free hand when you say "sit." If the dog moves away, you'll have to put the treat back in your pocket, hold the dog by the collar and then push the hindquarters down while giving the sit command. When the dog is sitting, give the treat as quickly as possible.

If your dog is a voracious eater, you can use a pellet of its regular dry food for the treat. If your dog is indifferent to its ordinary food, use a piece of packaged dog treats from the grocery store. You can even use packaged cat treats; dogs love the taste and smell of cat food. Commercial treats are much less sticky to carry in your pocket than are pieces of human food such as cubes of cheese.

When your dog sits on command most of the time, start reminding it each time that it does not sit promptly. With your hand that is not holding the treat, push down on the dog's rear end while saying "sit." Give the treat only when your dog is in the sitting position.

At first, teach your dog what sit means in a situation where it is not excited to see you. Teach "sit" in the kitchen, hallway, or yard. When the dog understands, use the command when it is likely to jump. Put some treats in your pocket and take one out before you approach the dog or open the door. Step away from the dog. Hold the treat up in the usual place above its head. Say "sit" and give the treat when the dog complies. It will take about two weeks before your dog will sit on command even when it is excited.

You won't have to use the treat for the rest of the dog's life to get it to sit. When your dog is obeying reliably, give the treat only every other time, then every third time, then only occasionally. If you bend over to pet the dog and say "good dog" when it sits, it will probably get up and jump on you again. Don't do it; walk away and ignore the dog until its desire to greet you by jumping has diminished.

Use adverse stimuli: the command "back!"

If your dog obeys the sit command at other times, but continues to ignore sit when it wants to jump on you, you will need to use something that will get its attention before it jumps. This is where the adverse stimulus is used. This is the application of something unpleasant that the dog will try to avoid. Use the command "back" and immediately follow the word by applying a correction that the dog will try to avoid.

Use a correction device to prevent your dog from jumping on you. A squirt from a can of compressed air works the best. The traditional correction is a swat with a rolled-up newspaper, but there are better things to use as a correction device. Objects that make a threatening noise or emit unpleasant spray make good tools for correcting your dog. The noise made by shaking an empty soda can containing a few pennies (tape over the opening) will stop some dogs from jumping. A toy water pistol is a good choice if your dog doesn't like to be squirted.

Devices that are advertised to stop barking can also be effective to stop jumping. Pet stores and pet supply catalogs offer gadgets that makes high-pitched irritating sounds intended to make dogs uncomfortable. There is a hand-held device with which you can squirt your dog with citronella oil. A very effective tool to stop a dog from jumping is a blast from a canister of compressed air. Cans of compressed air are used to blow the dirt out of delicate electronic equipment and are sold at computer stores to. If you use pressurized cans of any other material, for example air freshener, be very sure to aim above the dog's head. Tools such as these can be the bridge between being jumped on and a dog that greets you with all four paws on the floor.

Soon the word "back" will mean that a correction is imminent. Then you will not have to use the correction at all. Eventually you will not even have to use the command "back." You'll just say "sit," and your dog will comply.

Inappropriate greeting of guests.

Just because your dog greets you politely, don't assume that it will not jump on your guests. Dogs that are well trained not to jump on you may not apply that training to other people. Your dog is likely to leap all over strangers as though it had no training at all.

When people come to your home, take charge of your dog's behavior exactly as you did when it tried to jump on you. Command "back." Apply the correction if necessary. Give the command "sit." Give the reward when your dog complies. Be ready to do this before you open the door. Don't expect your dog to obey a stranger's command to sit; it's your dog and must look to you for guidance.

The opposite of the overly friendly dog is the suspicious or the downright hostile dog. A dog growling or barking at the door is an enormously effective deterrent to trespassers, salesmen and even your best friend.

Control the mildly suspicious barker just as you controlled the overly friendly one: first say "back" and use the correction if necessary. Then say, "sit.' Then give the reward.

If you think your dog might bite someone, it is best that you not depend on its training to override its guard dog instinct. Put the dog in its Safe Place, which we'll discuss later, before you open the door. A hostile dog can be a good thing in some circumstances. If you are suspicious of whoever is on the other side of the door, don't restrain the dog until you're sure.

My dog barks at people or cars.

If you live in apartments or close to neighbors, dogs that run from window to window and bark at movement or noise from outside can be a real problem. The watchdog instinct and the instinct to chase prey is the reason dogs behave that way; some dogs have a lot of this instinct and some dogs seem to have none.

Use what your dog already learned to stop the behavior: the command, "back." "Back" means many things to your dog. Apply the correction if necessary. Command "sit." Your dog can't run and bark while it is sitting. Once your dog has learned that a correction accompanies the word "back" you will find that "back" is a multipurpose command. In this context "back" means quit that.

My dog sneaks out of opened doors.

It is important to prevent your dog from trying to push past you whenever an outside door is opened. If your dog gets loose on the street, it is in grave danger of being lost, hit by a car, lost, or picked up by the dog warden.

You already know how to keep your dog from sneaking past you. Give the command "back" quickly followed by the correction. Soon all you'll do is to say, "back." Don't praise or reward your dog when it retreats: trying to sneak out is not a praiseworthy action.

Keeping your dog off the furniture.

It's easy enough to train a dog to stay off furniture when you are present: just yell "back" or "no" and yank it onto the floor. The dog will learn that getting on the furniture gets it a harsh word, and, if necessary, a little correction. It is an entirely different matter to depend on a dog to stay off the furniture when you are away.

The best thing to do is never to allow your dog to get on the furniture in the first place, so it won't realize that it can get up there. You might not have that option: either your dog came to you already accustomed to being on furniture, or your dog is smart enough to figure out how much more comfortable the sofa is than the floor.

Pet stores and catalogs sell products intended to keep your dog off furniture in your absence. There are dog gates that prevent access to selected areas. There are mats that give the trespasser a small electric shock and mats that are uncomfortable for a dog to lie on. There are commercial deterrent sprays that are supposed to smell bad and repel dogs. You might have to experiment to find out which method works best for your dog.

Devise your own methods to keep your dog off furniture. Newspapers spread on the cushions will discourage some dogs. A kitchen chair on its side on the favorite couch keeps most dogs off. Mousetraps are widely recommended to snap and frighten the dog when it jumps on furniture. Never use rat traps, and set mousetraps upside down; you want the trap to spring into the air and frighten your dog. You don't want to come home and find your dog with a mousetrap on its nose!

You really don't have to fuss about your dog getting up on furniture. Make it easy on yourself. Cover your dog's favorite chair with a washable throw or close the dog in a place where it can't get near the new sofa.

Keeping your dog out of trouble: the Safe Place.

"My dog is perfect—when I'm home. But when I leave it alone, it gets on the furniture, it chews the rug, it barks a lot. What can I do?"

Unless your dog is faultless in the house, you need to have a Safe Place or enclosure where it can't get into trouble. Never think of confining your dog as putting it in jail. Think of it as keeping the both the dog and the house safe from harm.

A useful Safe Place is a house-kennel or cage. "Oh, I wouldn't put my dog in a cage." This owner is anthropomorphizing, or considering the dog to have the same feelings and attitudes as a person. This owner would resent being locked in a cage. Therefore his dog must not be caged. This owner might be perfectly happy to see an infant in a playpen where it can't get hurt or pull down the drapes. In this respect, a dog is no different from a young child. Both need protection from their own inadvertent actions. A Safe Place keeps your dog safe and your house safe.

Wire cages.

Cages are easily moved and easily cleaned. Cages can be located in a kitchen, in a hallway, in a basement, in a heated garage, even in a bedroom. Cages come in many sizes and are constructed of many different materials. Most wire cages can be folded for storage.

Wire cages are much nicer as a Safe Place for a dog than are plastic airline kennels. The dog can see out in a wire cage and is not isolated from its surroundings. Wire cages are sold in every size imaginable. Select a cage for your dog that is high enough for the dog to stand up and long enough for it to lie down comfortably.

Cages are not inexpensive, but cages are much less costly than replacing a couch or buying new carpeting. Cages with thin wires are satisfactory for small dogs, but large active dogs will chew and bend the wires, destroy the cage, escape and injure themselves in the process. The strongest cages have small-square openings instead of wire bars.

Check the latch on the door before you buy a cage. Is it secure? Is it easy to open and close? Does it require two hands? Do you have to stoop over to close it? If you have a problem with the cage door, you may be able to replace the door or just the latch with something easier to use. One solution is replacing the entire door with a guillotine type door from a pet supply catalog. These guillotine doors are easy to attach to the front of many commercial cages. With a guillotine door, all you have to do to open or close the cage is lift up or lower a rope.

Other Safe Places.

A free standing chain-link pen in your basement or heated garage could be a perfect solution for your large, active dog. Pens are also not inexpensive, but can be worth the money for many years of secure confinement for your large dog. Chain link pens are made of four sections of fence with a gate in one section. The sections are joined at the corners with metal fasteners. These pens come in several sizes to fit in the selected space. You can buy these pens from hardware stores, pet stores, home improvement stores and pet catalogs. Some suppliers will deliver and perhaps even assemble your pen wherever you chose.

If you have a small dog, an exercise pen may be just what

you need for its Safe Place. Exercise pens are made of wire in joined sections that can be set up to form a square. They are made for exhibitors at dog shows to confine their entries, but can be used as a Safe Place in your home. Although they can be purchased in sizes for larger dogs, these pens are not sturdy enough to depend on them to confine anything bigger than a small terrier.

If you have a hallway or entrance way that would be convenient to use as your dog's Safe Place, you can buy a gate to confine the dog to that area. Pet supply catalogs are full of gates and barriers of every description, most of which can be adjusted to fit openings of various sizes. Some gates can be expanded to stay in place in a doorway. Some are intended to be mounted on walls or door frames. Whatever kind of gate you need, you can find it for sale in a catalog.

A small room such as a utility room can be entirely satisfactory as a Safe Place for any dog that is not too destructive. You can use a bedroom or even a bathroom if the dog is reasonably well behaved in there and will settle down and not destroy the furnishings.

"Yes, but my dog will scratch up the door if it's locked in there." You're right, it most likely will. Prevent damage by covering the bottom of the door with a surface that the dog cannot mar no matter how much it scratches.

There are several materials that will withstand years of serious scratching. Pick a hardware store or lumberyard that will cut the material to the size panel you need to fit the door. Ask to have a hole drilled in each corner so that you can screw the panel in place.

One-eighth-inch tempered Masonite is the least expensive and most easily obtained material to protect your door. Get only tempered Masonite and screw it to the door with the tempered side (the smooth dark side) out.

If you don't like the looks of a Masonite panel, you can buy a piece of clear plastic at a hardware store and have it cut to fit. Don't get the plastic used to replace glass in storm windows; it's not thick enough to protect against anything except the claws of a very small dog. If you prefer, you can use a large brass kick plate of the type used in commercial buildings.

Training your dog to enter the Safe Place.

"I can't get him to go in there." Sure you can. Just use your dog's favorite treat. Give it a piece so that it will be looking for more. Say, "kennel" (or "in") and toss a piece of the treat half way into the Safe Place. The dog will reach in for it. Toss the next treat farther back into the Safe Place. Leave the kennel door open and repeat enticing the dog to enter to get a treat. Close the kennel door only after the dog has gone inside for a treat several times.

If you are using a safe room, enter with the dog (with a treat if necessary) and make the dog stay in the room when you leave. If it tries to crowd past you to escape, use your command ("back") and give a correction just as you did when it tried to get out the front door.

Quiet, please! The no-bark collar.

"Yes, but my dog will bark all the time it's shut in its Safe Place." You're right, it might do that. You can ignore the noise until your dog gets tired of barking, which might take a very long time. Some dogs will never quit barking when confined to their Safe Places. Not only is the barking terribly annoying to you, your neighbors won't like it either.

Opening the door to the Safe Place and punishing the dog

for barking won't stop the barking for longer than it takes you to walk away. The dog barks because it doesn't want to be confined alone. When you open the door, the dog stops barking because it is no longer alone. If you punish it when it is not barking, it won't connect the punishment with the barking; it will connect the punishment with your arrival.

Shouting at the barking dog in its Safe Place without opening the door won't stop the barking. Your dog will soon learn that you aren't standing there all the time and will bark as soon as you walk away.

There is a way to silence every barking dog whenever necessary. The correct and humane use of a no-bark collar will stop every normal dog from barking until the collar is removed. The no-bark collar is a device that administers an unpleasant sensation to the dog whenever it barks. Some of these collars work by sensing the sound of the bark; some work by sensing the vibration made by the dog's vocal cords. Collars that work by sensing vibrations must fit snugly and the sensing device (the little box on the collar) must contact the dog's throat under its chin.

"Is it cruel to give your dog an unpleasant experience when it barks?" Isn't it much more cruel to have to give up your dog to an uncertain fate because of its barking? Wearing a no-bark collar, your dog gets a correction every time it barks. The dog learns very soon how to avoid the correction—it doesn't bark. The correction occurs whether or not you are present, so the dog never blames you for the unpleasant sensation.

Once trained to the no-bark collar, even a non-functioning collar will keep a dog quiet for days or weeks. Eventually the dog will seem to "forget" and will need a reminder. If the dog discovers that the collar no longer works, eventually it will start to bark again.

Pet stores, pet supply catalogs and hardware stores sell several types of no-bark collars. Some types of collars work better than other types. Some dogs require significantly unpleasant sensations to stop them from barking; some dogs merely need a little reminder to keep them quiet. Select a no-bark collar to fit your needs and the temperament of your barker.

The no-bark shock collar.

This collar consists of a battery enclosed in a little box attached to the collar. Two terminals on the underside of the box contact the skin of the dog's throat. When the dog barks, the vibrations close the circuit and the dog gets a little shock. Some of these collars have rechargeable batteries, some have replaceable batteries. The rechargeable kind cost more but may be less expensive to use than those that require frequent replacement of batteries.

Several manufacturers make no-bark shock collars. All no-bark collars come supplied with different lengths of screw-in terminals to contact the skin of dogs with different kind of hair coats. Some of these collars can be programmed to allow the dog a bark or two before they apply the shock. Some collars sound a warning noise before they shock. None of these fancy features is really necessary to keep a dog from barking, but all add to the cost of the collar. Buy the least expensive collar that will do your job.

No normal dog is going to continue to bark wearing a correctly used no-bark shock collar. The dog will bark once; try it again; maybe try it a third time; and become a reformed character. Even the worst, most constant barkers stop any and all barking within a few minutes of wearing these collars. If your dog continues to bark when wearing a no-bark shock collar, the collar is not working, the collar is not adjusted so that the terminals make contact with the dog's skin, or the shock level is set too low.

You must adjust the shock level of some no-bark shock collars. The level needed to stop a dog from barking depends on the temperament and determination of the dog. Unless you have a timid dog, don't start with the lowest level, which is a very mild shock. Your dog may learn to ignore the tiny shock and bark in spite of it. When you raise the shock level one more setting, your dog may learn to tolerate just a little more shock and continue to bark. If you gradually increase the shock level, you will be training your dog to tolerate the shock rather than to inhibit its barking.

For most dogs, start with a shock of sufficient strength to make it very unpleasant for it to bark. This will be in the upper third of the setting range. For a really determined barker, start with the highest shock level. After only a couple of unpleasant stimuli, your dog will realize that it receives a shock only when it barks. The result: peace and quiet.

At least one brand of no-bark collar adjusts the shock to the level that will cause the dog to stop barking. If the dog barks when it gets a tiny shock, the collar automatically raises the shock one level. These collars do the work for you.

The spray no-bark collar.

These collars look somewhat like the shock collars but they work entirely differently. When the dog barks, a spray of citronella oil is released in its face. The dog stops barking to avoid being startled by the spray and annoyed by the odor of citronella. People who object to giving a dog a small shock to prevent it from barking advocate the citronella spray collar.

Citronella oil is harmless but distasteful to dogs. A spray of citronella oil in the face will stop a dog's bark for a while. Eventually, some dogs get used to the spray, ignore it and continue to bark. It actually seems as though some dogs will bark at the spray. The spray no-bark collar costs about as much as a shock collar, and the spray collar (which also requires replacement batteries) must be refilled frequently from a container of citronella oil, which is not inexpensive.

The Sonic no-bark collar.

Two types of sonic collars are on the market. One is said to emit a high frequency tone "that only the dog can hear" when the dog barks. Dogs are supposed to be irritated by this tone and avoid the irritation by not barking. If the dog actually does hear the tone, it may ignore it as meaningless or annoying.

The other type of sonic no-bark collar emits an audibly loud sound to startle the dog into silence. These probably work better than the high frequency tone, at least for a while. Although the least expensive of all the no-bark collars, both of the sonic models are likely to be less effective than either the no-bark shock collar or the citronella spray collar.

None of the no-bark collars should be left on your dog all the time. Use these collars only when the dog's silence is important. If your dog barks when it is in its Safe Place, put the collar on when you put it in there. If your dog barks when you go away, put the collar on before you leave the house. If your dog barks in the yard and bothers the neighbors, put the collar on when you let it out. If your dog wears the collar only at special times, your dog soon will realize that's the time it must be quiet.

If you don't want to use a no-bark collar, you can buy other devices that irritate the barker with an unpleasant sound. Some of these are handheld, some you can mount on the wall near the barker's Safe Place. A little microphone in the device detects barking and sets off the sound. These probably won't work as consistently as a collar with a dedicated barker.

TED

The year I entered veterinary school, I paid my fees, bought my textbooks and scraped together some extra money to replenish my wardrobe. I bought two pairs of new shoes, one black, one brown. I figured that I'd be able to wear one or the other pair with everything I owned.

One evening, I heard a chewing sound coming from the bedroom. I went to investigate. My new shoes were on the floor. Ted, my perfectly behaved, obedience-trained, mature German Shepherd had chewed two shoes—one of each pair! I was able to repair the black shoe but I didn't wear any brown clothes during my entire freshman year.

How do I guard food, toys and areas?

Dogs may be possessive of their food, their toys, or their favorite chair. They snarl, bare their teeth, or actually snap if anyone gets too close to "their" property. This is a dominance issue—the dog considers itself to be the boss, or at least the owner of the protected object, and refuses to give it up.

What you do about your dog's attitude depends on your own attitude. It would be a lot of trouble (and some dogs will bite) to convince the dog that you're the boss in every situation. Make choices. Is it worth all that strife? Why not just avoid the issue whenever you can.

If your dog is very food-aggressive, put its food down in the usual place while the dog is somewhere else (outside, or in another room.) Let the dog in, allow it to eat its food undisturbed, call it out of the room and then take away the empty bowl. If you have two dogs, feed them in separate rooms. If the dog guards its toys, never give it food-like toys such as rawhide or pigs' ears. These will stimulate the same instinctive guarding behavior as does the dog's food. Allow other toys only if the dog doesn't display aggression when a person approaches within a few feet of the toy. Dogs can live without toys more successfully than persons can tolerate being bitten just for walking into a room where a dog is guarding a toy.

A very dominant dog may guard its sleeping place and snarl or snap whenever someone approaches. Be sure that this dog's sleeping place is not in a traffic pattern in the house where people have to walk close to it. If it is, move the dog's blanket or favorite chair to an out-of-the way place and prevent access to the old place until the dog is sleeping in the new location. Don't get bitten accidentally.

Occasionally a dog will get on a chair or bed and snarl when you try to remove it. It's very hard to have sympathy for this dog. Just use the all-purpose command, "back," and your spray canister as the correction method. Don't offer this dog a reward for obeying; it should not snarl at you under any circumstances.

My dog chews my personal belongings.

Many, many, many years ago, my mother taught me how to keep our dogs from chewing up my toys. "Put your things away," she advised. "You can't expect that dog to know what it's not supposed to chew." Mother's wisdom is just as applicable now as it was then.

A dog does not think like a person. Your dog won't know

the difference between its toys and your "toys," no matter how many bones or balls are lying around. Advice such as "put Tabasco sauce on things to make them taste bad," or "say 'no' When your dog even looks at a forbidden object" isn't likely to change a dog's behavior when you aren't present to correct it. Take your mother's advice and pick up your stuff.

A good alternative to picking up your "toys" is to put your dog in its Safe Place whenever you have to be absent. Put some dog toys in the Safe Place with your dog so that it will have something that it is permitted to chew.

My dog steals food.

The dog that snatches food off the kitchen counter and the dog that cleans your plate when you get up to answer the phone is a dog obeying its strongest survival instincts: eat whatever you can get. It is not reasonable to expect an animal to ignore this instinct. This instinct can be modified but not erased.

You probably can convince your dog not to steal food while you are present. Say "no" or "back" and, if necessary, use your sonic noisemaker, compressed air canister, soda can full of pennies, or whatever device you used to keep your dog from jumping on you. But when you are going to be out of the room, don't leave food in your dog's reach. Put your dinner on top of the refrigerator to defrost, not on the kitchen counter.

Chapter 2
Housebreaking Your Dog

Cookie was nothing but a hound dog. She was a very sad little hound dog indeed, peering out at me through the wires of her cage. She was small for a beagle, brown and black, with white around the muzzle revealing her age. Her puzzled expression and slowly wagging tail said it all "Why am I here? Why aren't I home with my family? When will someone come for me?"

Cookie is the kind of relinquishment that all humane societies dread. A sweet, shy old dog that wouldn't harm a fly, she wanted nothing but to lick her owner's hand in thanks for a bowl of dog food and a soft resting place, but Cookie was on death row.

I asked the shelter manager where Cookie had come from. "Some older man and his daughter turned her in yesterday. I think the man was crying when they left." The director handed me Cookie's intake papers. The reason for relinquishment: can't keep her. Messes in the house every night.

Those few words said it all. Maybe because of her age, maybe because of some change in diet or routine, Cookie had taken to eliminating in the house at night. The older gentlemen might be living with his daughter or might have been persuaded by the daughter that a dog that ever messes in the house is an unacceptable, unsanitary pet. He was given no choice but to leave his old friend to her fate at the shelter.

Cookie was going to die. Nobody adopts old dogs that mess in the house, the shelter manager reminded me. They couldn't very well fail to inform prospective adopters of Cookie's problem. If they didn't mention it, the adopters would soon find out and Cookie would be returned after a couple of nights. Might as well euthanize her and get it over with.

Personally, I find it hard to equate in-house elimination with a capital offense. It's not nice, it's unsanitary, it's smelly and it can ruin carpets, but should "accidents" cause a dog to be put to death?

Neither is "getting rid of the dog" an acceptable solution. We might save our carpets, but at the terrible expense of losing our good friend and companion. And the dog that is "gotten rid of" is almost certain to continue its ways in another home and eventually end up homeless, abandoned and euthanized. No, there are better ways to control these problems.

Dogs' instincts make housebreaking possible.

We've all read the theory behind housebreaking dogs: dogs are a den-dwelling species and instinctively want to keep their living quarters clean. Unfortunately, dogs don't instinctively want to keep our much more spacious living quarters clean. They must be taught to do so if they are to be acceptable house pets. When they fail to learn this lesson completely, or when a physical or behavioral problem causes them to forget their learned inhibitions, those discouraging housebreaking mistakes occur.

My dog moves its bowels in the house.

"Why? How can I stop this?" You may not be taking the dog out at the right time. The most common reason for a dog to defecate in the house is lack of access to the correct area when it needs to defecate.

In all animals, the filling of the stomach by eating stimulates the large intestine to empty. Veterinarians (and human physicians) call this the gastrocolic reflex. Think of it this way: food in, waste out. This reflex is strong in animals such as dogs and humans that consume their food at intervals. Grazing animals, such as horses and cattle that eat almost continuously, have weak gastrocolic reflexes and defecate repeatedly.

Of course, adult humans don't run to the bathroom the minute they swallow their last bite. Infants, however, often need to be changed just after they finish their meal. By the time a child is two or three years old, he has developed the reflex inhibition called "toilet training"; he has learned to wait until he is in the right place to defecate and to ask to be taken to the right place when he feels the need. The child, just like the housebroken dog, develops voluntary control over that body function.

Adult humans will inhibit bowel movements for a long time. Some adult dogs will, too. Some dogs won't, which is when the dog defecates in the house. Housebreaking consists of inhibiting the reflex and teaching bowel control until the dog gets to the "bathroom." An otherwise healthy dog that doesn't wait until it is taken out has poorly developed reflexes to inhibit its bowel movements.

Use the gastrocolic reflex to your advantage.

See that your dog is able to get to the proper "bathroom" spot within a short time after you feed it. A few dogs will defecate just before they eat; their gastrocolic reflex is stimulated by the anticipation of food. If yours is one of these, take it out first, then feed it, then just to be sure, take it out again.

Avoiding accidents through proper feeding.

Yes, but my dog moves its bowels at other times, too. Yes, of course it does. Right after eating is not the only time a dog feels the need to defecate. Other reflexes cause a dog to move its bowels when its large intestine is full. Food takes 12 hours or more to pass through a dog's intestinal tract. This means that the residue of the food you gave your dog at 5 PM will be fecal material and ready to be passed at approximately 5 AM, a time when few dogs have access to the outdoors. Twelve hours is very general estimate, and depends on the individual dog, its diet and its exercise schedule. With a little experimenting to find out when your dog will defecate, it is possible to arrange its feeding and exercise schedule so that it won't move its bowels when and where it shouldn't. Since the estimate of 12 hours between food in-feces out is very general, you will have to experiment to get the schedule exactly right.

Arrange your dog's feeding time so it is convenient for you to get it out when it will naturally have a bowel movement. If you feed at eight in the morning, it will probably defecate after eating and need to go out again between six and nine at night. If you feed at 5 PM, the dog's bowel will be full and it will need to defecate between three and six in the morning. Your housebroken dog is able to inhibit this reflex and wait until you get up and take it out. The dog that does not inhibit the reflex is the one that messes on the floor at night.

Do some experiments. Feed the evening meal at 7 PM and

take the dog out at 7:15. Your dog probably will defecate at that time, and be able to wait until you get up in the morning and take it out before it moves its bowels again. If your dog still makes mistakes, try feeding it an hour or two earlier or later.

Adult dogs do well with one feeding a day, but many owners feel better about feeding twice a day. If your dog has good bowel control (good reflex inhibition) and you are able to take it out several times a day, your dog will appreciate two meals a day. If you have any problems with your healthy dog defecating in the house, you probably can solve them with a correctly timed single feeding a day.

I have two dogs. How can I tell which one's the culprit?

Two dogs of similar size will have similar-sized bowel movements. Which one is making the mess? It even could be both of them at different times. If you can confine the dogs to separate areas in the house, you can answer the question that way. If you arrange the feeding schedules of both dogs so that they defecate at the proper time, you might not even need to detect the culprit.

A preschool teacher who had this problem discovered which dog was messing in the house in a very unique way. She knew that children's crayons are non-toxic (kids nibble them) so she shredded a small yellow crayon stub and added it to the food of one of her dogs. The guilty dog was discovered when she saw yellow crayon bits in its stool.

How do I prevent and control my dog's diarrhea?

Diarrhea is defined as the passing of unformed stools. If

your dog has loose or watery stools, there's a medical cause for the condition. As with other animals, diarrhea can cause temporary loss of bowel control.

Occasional diarrhea in the dog is most often caused by overfeeding or by eating unusual items such as large amounts of table scraps or garbage. The dog that has diarrhea but is normally active and wants to eat is seldom a very sick dog; it just has eaten something that disagrees with it. The simple and effective treatment for occasional diarrhea is to skip a feeding—or two feedings, if the dog's intestinal tract is really upset. If you feel guilty about not feeding your dog at its regular mealtime, feed it only a quarter of its normal amount. Let its intestines rest and recover.

A dog that has diarrhea almost all of the time has a medical problem. Take a small sample of a fresh stool to your veterinarian to have the stool examined for abnormalities and parasites. A good fecal sample should be smaller than a golf ball and contained in a small paper cup, empty jar, or similar container.

> Internal parasites are a frequent cause of diarrhea and mistakes in puppies, but an adult dog must have a heavy load of "worms" to cause diarrhea. A veterinarian or a veterinary technician can conduct a microscopic examination of your dog's fecal material and find the cause. Then a veterinarian can prescribe medication specifically for the parasite that is affecting your dog.

> A deficiency in digestive enzymes may cause your dog to be unable to digest its food properly. Chronic diarrhea may be the result. Veterinarians are able to diagnose these problems and prescribe replacement enzymes that can be added to your dog's food.

> Overfeeding or feeding dog food to which the dog has a sensitivity may be the culprit. A simple change in diet may be all that is needed.

> Damage to a dog's intestinal tract from chemical or mechanical irritants. The dog that has eaten harsh foreign material, for example a steel-wool pad, not only will have diarrhea, but will have intestinal pain and will refuse to eat. Take the dog to a veterinarian as soon as possible.

> Some virus diseases of dogs cause the problem. The dog that is suffering from a viral disease may not only have diarrhea, but may have blood in its stools or tarry stools. These dogs are obviously sick and must see a veterinarian as soon as possible.

My dog doesn't seem to know when it is defecating.

The dog drops fecal material onto the floor and doesn't seem to be aware that it is doing it may have an injury or deformity in its spine. Accidents, spinal malformations, or abnormal bony growths could cause this problem.

Structural defects of the spine are inherited in certain breeds. The inherited conditions do not appear until the dog is middle-aged or older. To obtain a diagnosis of this problem will require X-rays of the dog's entire spine, including its neck. Fortunately, this problem is relatively rare. Treatment of these conditions often is not effective.

My dog is urinating in the house.

Dogs and other animals have to urinate when their bladders are full. Bladders get full when kidneys produce enough urine to fill them. Dogs don't drink coffee, soft drinks, or beer all day; a normal dog drinks only the amount of water that is required by its body. Normal dogs' kidneys produce enough urine to require a healthy dog to empty its bladder only three or four times a day. A dog with unhealthy kidneys or bladder may have to relieve itself many more times in a 24-hour period. Such a dog will have to urinate at times other than it regular trips outside.

Behavioral reasons are common causes of your dog urinating in the house, but before you get angry at it, be sure that the dog has a healthy urinary tract. Your dog may have a disease of the kidneys or bladder if:

> It suddenly began to urinate in the house. Does your dog want to go outside all the time?
> It is always thirsty. Is its water bowl is frequently empty?
> Its urine is cloudy or dark, or you can see blood in it.

Never withhold water from a dog except on the advice of a veterinarian. If your dog has abnormal kidney function, it must have extra water to remove waste products from its body.

Does your dog strain to urinate, or seem to take a long time to urinate? Does your older spayed female dogs urinate in her sleep, apparently without knowing that she's doing it? This condition is often from bladder sphincter weakness and can be treated with medication.

These signs, especially in middle-aged or older dogs, may indicate kidney disease, diabetes, bladder disease, bladder stones, or other disease conditions of the kidneys and bladder. If you suspect that your dog has a physical problem, or even if you think its urinating in the house is entirely behavioral, it is wise to make sure and have its urine examined by a veterinarian. Just as in human medicine, a complete urinalysis is often diagnostic of many medical conditions.

How can I get a urine sample from my dog?

This isn't always easy, but it is always necessary to determine the conditions of a dog's kidneys and bladder. If you can take a sample to the veterinarian, you may expedite the diagnosis and treatment of your dog's problem.

The easiest way to collect a dog's urine sample is to hold a pan in the appropriate place when the dog urinates. A disposable aluminum pie pan is a good container in which to collect a urine sample. The sample need not be more than a couple of teaspoonfuls of urine. Most dogs will have to be on a leash for you to get close enough to collect its urine. It might be easier for you to collect urine from your dog first thing in the morning, when it hasn't urinated all night. It's easier to collect urine from a male dog than from a female; you have to push the pan under the female at just the right time.

After you have collected the sample, pour it into a clean jar with a lid. Don't use a jar that could have traces of jam, jelly, or honey in it—the urine might accidentally test positive for sugar. If you can't get the sample to your veterinarian within a couple of hours, cover the jar and refrigerate it until you can take it for examination.

Your veterinarian will examine the urine for sugar, protein, specific gravity (to check kidney function) and look at the urine under the microscope for crystals, blood cells, abnormal tissue cells and other indications of disease. Many conditions can be ruled in or out from a complete urinalysis.

Once your veterinarian has diagnosed the problem, he or she will be able to recommend appropriate treatment. Further tests such as radiographs may be required for some diagnoses. In some cases, the veterinarian may recommend that the dog be referred to a specialist.

BRANDY

The devoted owner of Brandy, a six-month-old golden retriever, had an appointment for a rabies vaccine, but that was not the real reason for the visit. The owner had other issues in mind.

"Doctor, she squats and urinates all the time. She doesn't seem to be able to help herself. Is this normal?"

I immediately thought of the submissive urination of puppies, when they are so excited to see their owners that they simply loose control. I asked, "Does she do this when you come home? When she's excited to see you?

"No, no—she might do it at any time." Just as her owner spoke, Brandy squatted and produced a huge puddle right in front of us. "See, just like that."

I immediately took out a paper indicator strip and dropped it into the puddle. Everything was normal. I retrieved a sample of the urine and checked the water content. Brandy's urine was very diluted. I started to explain about the possibility of some sort of kidney malfunction when a thought occurred to me. "What do you feed her?" I asked.

"Just dog food." The owner named a premium brand.

"Do you feed it dry or do you moisten it?"

"Oh, the food looks so unappetizing when it's dry. I always moisten it with water and I add a couple of chicken bouillon cubes so she will like it better."

Immediately, we had the solution to Brandy's problem. The owner wanted to feed her dog something tasty and didn't realize that the bouillon contained a huge amount of salt. The salt made Brandy thirsty and she drank a great deal of water. The water had to go somewhere, so it went onto the floor.

Your dog may be urinating in the house because of behavioral problems.

Too often a dog urinates in the house without any signs of illness at all. The dog is taken out frequently, its urinalysis is normal and no physical problems can be found. This is a very disturbing situation; your old buddy is not a clean pet.

Your dog may be marking its territory with the scent of its urine. The dominant male member of a pack of wild canines instinctively defines its territory by urinating on upright objects in the area. The distinctive scent of its urine is a warning to other wild dogs "this is my home. Stay away!"

Unfortunately, domestication has not removed this instinct from our house pets. Scent marking is the most common reason for healthy mature dogs' urinating in the house. The instinct to scent-mark is promoted by sex hormones. The worst culprits are un-neutered sexually mature male dogs. Female dogs that are not spayed might scent-mark, too, but much less often than un-neutered males.

The male dog that scent-marks lifts its leg and squirts small amounts of urine on many surfaces in the house. It prefers upright objects such as drapes, upholstered furniture and the bottoms of bedspreads. The rare female backs up to these objects when she scent-marks.

A dog that is neutered or spayed before it reaches puberty almost never develops the scent-marking habit. Most dogs reach puberty at six to nine months of age, but the age of puberty in dogs is quite variable, just as it is in humans.

A dog that has developed the habit of scent-marking seldom reforms immediately after it is surgically neutered or spayed. Expect some improvement, if you're lucky, a few weeks or months after the surgery. Other behavioral reasons that cause dogs to urinate in the house are:

> Your dog may not be completely housebroken. Some dogs are just not good at being housebroken. A few dogs don't seem to care where they urinate. Some dogs will sneak into another room and wet where the owner can't see them do it. For these problems, appropriate confinement in a Safe Place, as described in Chapter 1, is the way to improve the dog's habits, or at least to prevent damage.

> Your old dog may be getting forgetful. Veterinarians call this "age-associated cognitive dysfunction." Medication prescribed for this sort of problem seldom helps much. You might need to keep your older dog in its Safe Place on newspapers when you are not at home.

"Spite marking" (urinating or defecating in the house when you leave it home alone) is a false concept. It doesn't do it to spite you. The dog's reflexes simply are not being inhibited by the owner's presence, or the dog has been confined for too long to be able to control its reflexes.

How can I keep my dog from making housebreaking mistakes?

Unless you catch your dog in the act, there is no use to punish it for messing in the house. Even if you "show" it the mistake later, the dog will have absolutely no idea of why it is being punished. Your aim must be to prevent the problem rather than cure it. Here are a few ways.

> Confine your dog in its Safe Place (when appropriate) to prevent damage to your home.

> Adjust your dog's feeding time and exercise routine. Ex-

periment until you find the best results.

> Have your dog neutered or spayed before it reaches puberty. If it is already an adult, have it neutered or spayed as soon as possible.

> Be sure your dog has no medical reasons for its mistakes and have it treated if necessary.

Just in case: how to remove feces, urine, odors and stains from just about anything.

Animals and children can be expected to have "accidents." Messes on floors are unpleasant, but not a tragedy. We need to find ways to get the material up and the surfaces restored as quickly, easily and completely as possible. The tools you may need include:

> Scraper. A small plastic windshield scraper is good for this purpose and the best thing for use on wood floors and surfaces that scratch easily; a 4-inch steel paint scraper is more effective for use on carpets.

> Paper towels, lots of them.

> Scrub brush and an old tooth brush.

> Newspapers to wrap the waste in for disposal.

> Mop. Common cellulose sponge mops are not very effective in removing all liquids from un-carpeted surfaces. Often the surface needs to be dried with a cloth or another mop. String mops are not easy to clean. The most effective mop is made by Rubbermaid of blue rubber, has a black plastic handle and a lever for easy squeeze-out. This mop leaves any un-carpeted surface nearly dry.

> All-purpose household cleaner in a spray bottle.

> Enzyme cleaner. Many such products are on the market.

Most are very effective in removing odors and stains. The enzymes in the products literally digest organic waste material. Pet supply stores and catalogs are full of these products; you can even buy them at the grocery store.

> Commercial carpet cleaning products. These are designed to be used with a steam-cleaning carpet machine. They are not very practical for use in cleaning up the occasional mess.

> Air spray for odor control. Any kind you find the least offensive. You can spray it in the air; since air sprays contain no pigment, you can spray a little on the affected area.

Pick it up! Scrape it up! Blot it up! Mop it up!

This may be an unsavory topic, but it can be vital information. The right tools, procedures and products can make a really big mess disappear quickly, easily and completely.

Fecal material and vomit on carpeting and rugs.

Formed feces are the easiest to remove. Simply pick them up with a paper towel or toilet paper, being careful not to accidentally rub the fecal material into the carpet. Flush the feces and paper down the toilet and inspect the surface for residue. Hard feces may not leave a trace. A squirt of air spray and you're done.

Soft feces will leave some material on the surface of the carpet. Loose feces such as diarrhea and vomited material will leave quite a bit more. Carefully pick up all that you can with a paper towel. Then use the scraper to remove as much of the rest as possible. Scrape in the direction of the nap of the carpet.

Spray the area lightly with the all-purpose spray cleaner. Dip your scrub brush in water and scrub the area in the direction of the nap. Repeat the spraying and scrubbing as many times as needed to remove all traces of the material. Unless there is a lot of mess remaining after you have scraped up all you can, three or four scrubs will usually remove the remaining material. If any remains, use an enzyme cleaner to destroy it.

Rinse the brush between scrubs and finish with a couple of scrubs using only plain water. Finish by covering the area with an old towel or several layers of paper towels and stamping on them to blot up as much water as possible. Change the towels several times, until no more fluid is absorbed. Allow the carpet to dry and raise the nap by vacuuming.

If you have no all-purpose spray, you can use dishwasher detergent very sparingly. Put a little detergent onto the brush, dip the brush in water and scrub. Don't squirt the detergent directly from the bottle onto the carpeting; you'll never get all the suds out of the carpet and you will leave a light spot of suds that will show even when the area is dry.

Scrub an area a little larger than necessary to prevent lines of demarcation from showing. Light colored carpeting may require more scrubbing and rinsing to completely remove all signs of the material.

An unfortunate side-effect of scrubbing spots off carpeting may be a clean place in an otherwise not-so-clean carpet. Unless your carpet is snow white, don't apply any kind of bleach, and never use chlorine bleach on natural fibers. A hole in the carpet is worse than a spot.

If area rugs get messed on, scrub off the material just as if it were on carpeting. Spots on these rugs are removed more completely (and less expensively) by scrubbing with detergent and water than they are by professional dry cleaning. In good weather, you can lay area rugs out on the driveway or hang them on a fence, scrub them, rinse them with a hose and leave them out until they are dry.

Washable throw rugs are the easiest to clean. Simply scrape off as much as you can and toss them into the washer.

GYPSY

Should the love for his dog be such a moving emotion that the owner makes major changes in his life? Perhaps this story shouldn't be told, but this is what happened.

Joe Hobbs was as careful as he could be about Gypsy getting out of the yard, but Mrs. Hobbs didn't share her husband's interest in the dog. One day when the gate was accidentally left open, Gypsy escaped and was hit by a car. Fortunately she wasn't killed, but she was badly hurt.

X-rays showed that the Hobbs' 4-year-old part-poodle had a broken pelvis and damage to her sacrum, the lower portion of her spine just before her tail. Fortunately the broken parts weren't far out of line and she didn't require major orthopedic surgery to put her back together. With proper treatment, Gypsy healed and was able to walk and run without pain just as she did before the accident.

But Gypsy's spinal nerves were damaged. She lost control of her bowels—fecal material just dropped out onto the floor. Gypsy didn't even know when she was defecating. I explained to the very concerned owners that the condition was not life threatening and that Gypsy's bowel control would probably improve with time. I didn't give it much thought after that.

On a Saturday morning about two weeks later, I saw an appointment for "Gypsy Hobbs" followed by the dreaded notation "euthanasia."

Joe came in carrying Gypsy. The dog was happily wagging her tail, but Joe looked terrible. He was obviously under severe emotional stress. He put Gypsy on the table and looked at me with teary eyes. "I guess we got to do it, Doc."

"But these cases usually get better. Don't you see any improvement?" I asked. "She looks good. Can't she run and play?"

"Yeah, she's fine, except for—well, you know. I don't think it's so bad—all I have to do is to pick up after her with a paper towel once in a while. But Phyllis says she won't have that dog messing all over."

Gypsy will get better in time," I assured him. "She may get over it entirely."

"That's what I told Phyllis. But she won't listen—says she won't have dog poop all over her house. Says it's either her or the dog. So, Doc, what can I do?"

"Well, I'd..." Suddenly I realized I'd better keep my feelings to myself and not say a thing. Maybe Joe Hobbs read my mind.

We stood there, staring at each other for a long minute. Gypsy licked her owner's hand. Abruptly, Joe picked up his dog, said "Yeah, Doc. Thanks." He turned and carried Gypsy out of the examination room.

Gypsy eventually regained most of her former bowel control. She was a regular patient at our practice for 10 more years. And the second Mrs. Hobbs loved the dog and was careful to never leave the gate open.

Urine on carpeting and rugs.

This is the worst cleaning job you're likely to encounter. With urine on carpets, speed is important. You must try to get urine out of carpets before it has time to penetrate to the lower levels of the surface and into the carpet padding. Once urine is in the padding, it will take more time and effort to remove it.

As soon as you see urine on a carpet, blot up as much as possible by covering the area with several layers of paper towels and stamping on them hard to soak up the urine. Change the towels several times, until no more moisture appears on the paper towels when you press them into the carpet.

Then proceed with the same method you used with fecal messes. Scrub the area with household cleaner and water. Rinse several times. Blot up as much water as possible by stamping on paper towels again. Let the area dry and vacuum up the carpet nap.

Complete removal of urine that has soaked deep into carpets is a difficult job. Even if the area looks and smells completely clean to us, the lingering odor may be enough to encourage a dog to eliminate there again.

Various household products have been recommended to neutralize urine odors in carpeting. White vinegar, which is a weak acid, and ammonia, which is alkaline, are the two most often mentioned. The pH (acidity or alkalinity) of dog urine depends on the dog's diet; most commercial dog foods cause urine to be alkaline. Since vinegar is an acid, it would be the logical choice to use to neutralize the urine. A much better choice is a commercial enzyme product made especially for pet urine in carpets. The procedure for use of enzymes is printed on the package of each product. In general, you have to apply enough of a solution of the product to penetrate to the depth of the urine deposit, allow it to dry and often repeat the process a few times. The enzyme literally "digests" residual urine and will remove the odors if the enzyme solution is used repeatedly.

Messes on un-carpeted surfaces.

Feces and urine on un-carpeted surfaces are usually easy to remove. For fecal material, pick up as much as you can with a paper towel, wipe up the rest with a damp paper towel, spray with household cleaner and wipe again. For urine, mop up the puddle with the rubber mop, rinse the mop and mop again.

Natural wood floors may need a little more care to protect the surface. Be careful with strong cleaners that may remove the wax. Use your spray cleaner only if plain water will not completely remove the material. Wipe up the cleaner as quickly as possible. Rinse and dry with a mop or more paper towels. Water allowed to remain on wood flooring may cause discoloration.

Composition flooring such as linoleum, asphalt tile and the new synthetic "wood" flooring usually clean up very easily. Ceramic tile is a problem only if material remains in the grout between the tiles. Use an old toothbrush to scrub stained grout with powdered cleanser. Bleach can be used on badly stained grout. The scrubbed areas may need to be re-sealed with commercial sealer after they are dry.

Upholstered furniture and curtains are seldom soiled with feces, but often soiled with urine from dogs that "mark." Incontinent dogs and spayed older females that "leak" in their sleep may be very damaging to chairs and couches. If your dog has these problems, it's best to keep it off the furniture. If you can't, try covering its favorite chair with a rubber sheet, or even a plastic shower curtain.

You'll have to scrub urine-stained upholstery by hand, using lots of household cleaner. If you use laundry or dish soap, it may be impossible to get all the suds out. Follow the scrubbing with the use of an enzyme cleaner. Slipcovers can be removed from the furniture, washed in the washer, or dry cleaned. Floor-length drapes, which are often the target of marking dogs, can be handled the same way as slipcovers. Personally, I shortened all my long drapes to windowsill-length.

What happened to Cookie?

Remember Cookie, the little old beagle who was headed for euthanasia just because she was no longer clean in the house at night? You will be happy to hear that Cookie is alive and well and has a new home.

Poor Cookie really didn't have a problem; her owners did. They could not be convinced that some slight change to her routine was all that was needed to prevent her from that undesirable behavior.

Shelter workers are suckers for helpless little animals. If they weren't, they would find easier, better-paying jobs. Fortunately, the little old dog caught the attention of a one of these workers who didn't believe that house-soiling is a capital offense.

The shelter worker made two small changes in Cookie's routine: she is fed only in the evening, because trials showed that she'd eliminate before bedtime and wouldn't again until morning. She also she sleeps in her Safe Place, a cage, just to be sure that there are no more "accidents" on the floor. Cookie has a soft blanket and a bowl of water in her cage. She is a delightful little pet and a great companion for her new owners.

Chapter 3
Disobedience in the Yard

Your dog needs to go outside for two reasons: to allow it to eliminate and to give it exercise. Your yard usually is your dog's "bathroom." The street is your dog's "gymnasium."

Most dogs need to go out in the yard several times a day: first thing in the morning, at noon, after it is fed and just before bedtime. Unless you prefer to stand outside with Princie on a leash, you need to set up some sort of fence or chain to keep the dog on the premises.

Can my dog run loose?

No dog should ever run loose without supervision! If you open the door and let Princie out alone, you're demonstrating that you don't really care about Princie's companionship, his health, or his very life. Even in rural areas, Princie can meet with disaster and never be seen again.

"But he always comes back." "Always" is a very long time, almost as long as "never." One day, Princie won't come back. The neighbors will find his crushed body in a ditch. Or he will jump into the car of the first person that calls to him. Or he will get far from home, be unable to find his way back, and starve. Is it worth the chance? Certainly, you value Princie more than that

"But I can't afford a fence." You don't have to have a fence. In fact, in some cases a chain is preferable. Princie can't climb over or dig under a chain as he could a fence. If you have enough money to buy dog food, you have the few dollars you'll need to buy the right collar and chain to keep your dog safe.

"But it's hard for me to put him on the chain." Keep reading. You'll learn easy ways to handle this problem.

Should my dog wear a collar in the house?

Your dog should wear a collar and identification tag at all times. In spite of your best intentions, your dog may get loose from your control and may disappear. If it has legible identification including a telephone number on its collar, your dog's chances of being returned are greatly increased. Even if your dog ends up at the dog warden, if your telephone number is on its collar you are likely to be called to come reclaim it (and pay a fine.)

You can buy a tag with your name and address on it from many sources. Hardware and pet stores often have coupons that you can fill out and mail away for tags. Some pet stores and animal shelters even have tag-making machines and can provide your dog with identification on the spot. Several sources are listed in the appendix.

Many dog tags are made with the dog's name at the top of the tag. When I order tags, I have the word "REWARD" printed on them instead of the dog's name. No, my dogs aren't all named Reward; that's just an added incentive for a finder to call me.

The identification tag can be attached to your dog's collar

either with rivets or with a metal "S" hook. All it takes is a pair of pliers.

In an emergency, or until your dog's tag arrives in the mail, you can write your telephone number on its collar with an indelible marker. This works best if your dog wears a light-colored flat nylon collar.

The regular leash with a snap.

Princie sees you approach with the leash. Oh, boy, we're going outside, he thinks. He starts for the door. You reach for his collar, but he's jumping around and won't hold still to allow you to put on the leash. There is a simple way to solve this problem. Convince your dog that nothing exciting is going to happen when the leash is attached. Put the leash on and take it off many times when you are not going anywhere, so that the dog doesn't associate the leash with an exciting event. Attach and remove the leash in several rooms, starting with a room away from the door. Leave the leash on the dog a varying amount of time-a few seconds to a couple of minutes. Within a few days, the dog will learn that the leash doesn't mean that there is anything exciting coming up.

When you are actually going to take the dog out, attach its leash in a room away from the exit. You may have to reinforce calm behavior by occasionally attaching the leash at random intervals throughout the dog's life.

Do you have a hard time to grasp the little ring on the collar where the leash is to be attached? Get a 3-inch snap from the hardware store. Clip this snap to the ring on the collar and leave it there. When you want to put your leash on the dog's collar, you can hold that extra snap like a handle. All you have to do is to grab the extra snap and attach the leash snap to the open end of the extra snap.

Another way to make it easy to attach Princie's leash is to get a large metal ring, either round or D-shape, and pass the collar through the ring before you buckle it onto your dog. It will be quite easy to grasp this loose ring and snap the leash onto it. Don't use a key ring unless you have a very small dog. A larger dog can pull a key ring apart.

Noose-type leash.

You can buy nylon dog leashes that have no snap, only a ring on one end and a hand loop on the other. To use a noose leash, you pass the body of the leash through the ring to make a loop that you slip over the dog's head.

Noose leashes are easy to put on, but they don't give much control over large or medium-sized dogs. The noose doesn't stop a strong dog from pulling on the leash, and when slack is allowed in the leash, the noose can open and allow the dog to escape. It's not a good idea to take a strong dog out of doors with only a noose leash.

If you have real difficulty restraining your dog, or if your dog ignores you, you can use a noose leash as a temporary device. Put the noose over the dog's head to give you something to hold it with while you move it, attach its regular leash, or put other control equipment on your dog.

You can make an emergency control device out of a regular leash: pass snap end through the hand loop to make a noose and put the noose over dog's head. You'll control the dog by holding the snap end of the leash.

I Have a fenced yard.

When you let Princie out in the fenced enclosure, he makes

a mad dash for the outer limits, barking furiously at passing cars and annoying the neighbors. When you leave him outside, he tries to crawl under or climb over the fence. He destroys any plants in the area. He digs his own foxholes, which become mud puddles when it rains. He ignores your calling him back inside and avoids your grasp when you try to catch him.

You may not have any problems at all with Princie's outdoor activities. You can open the door and let him out. You call "Princie, come!" and your dog will come in when it is time. If that's your situation, you are fortunate. Many dogs aren't that well behaved when they are loose in a fenced-in yard.

My dog won't come out of the yard when I call.

This is easiest behavior problem to eliminate. Bribe your dog. Get some absolutely delicious treats, like slices of hot-dog or pieces of boiled liver. Let Princie know that you have a handful of goodies. Go out in the yard and give him a bite. Stand near the door or the gate and give him another. Stand just inside the door or gate, and call "Princie, come!" Give him another treat. If your fenced yard adjoins your house, stand further inside the house and repeat the command "come!" followed by the treat. If your yard is a long distance from the house, slip your noose leash over Princie's head before you give him the treat.

You might have to use up a dozen treats before Princie learns that he gets a reward for coming when called. Eventually, and it may take two or three days, Princie will come for his treat when you hold open the door or come to the gate. You don't have to give the reward forever; when Princie responds correctly most of the time, reinforce the behavior by giving Princie a reward only occasionally.

Caution. Just because Princie comes to you when he is in your fenced yard, do not assume that he will obey if he is out-of-doors but not behind the fence. Princie may see other things more attractive to him than the reward, and he may run off.

My dog digs in the yard.

Will he dig under the fence? Does your dog dig unsightly holes in the yard? Do these holes become mud puddles every time it rains? Unfortunately, this is a habit for which there is no good cure.

Your dog digs holes in the yard because it's fun to dig and he has nothing better to do. If you get him another dog for a playmate, they both may dig. If you put all sorts of toys out there for your dog to play with, he may ignore them and dig anyway. The best answer seems to be to allow the dog loose in the yard for elimination only, call him in when he is done, and give him his exercise (and yours) on the end of a leash.

Fences for dogs must, of course, reach completely to the ground to prevent the dog from trying to crawl under them. A few dogs will dig at the fence line until they are able to squeeze under and escape. Most dogs can be discouraged from doing this by placing a barrier of large rocks or logs around the bottom of the fence.

My dog jumps or climbs over the fence.

The standard dog fence is usually four feet high. Few dogs can jump over a four-foot fence, but very active medium and large dogs can climb four feet, and some will climb six feet. It's not the huge breeds that climb; they're too heavy and not as agile as some of the relatively smaller dogs. For example, a fence that will hold a shepherd or a Doberman may not be much of a barrier to a pointer or a Dalmatian.

A dog learns to climb a fence by running at the fence, leaping part of the way up, getting his hind toes in the openings of the fence, and scrambling the rest of the way. Once a dog has learned that he can climb a fence, it is very difficult to prevent him from doing so. Some owners have installed electrically charged wires at the top of their fences. The kind that is made to keep rabbits out of gardens produces only a small shock and works well for the purpose. If all else fails, Princie might have to be allowed outside only on a chain. Be sure that the length of the chain will not allow him to climb the fence and be hanged.

My dog runs along the wire fence and barks.

Your dog does this because he sees (or thinks he sees) something outside of the fence that is interesting. It's usually the neighbors or passing cars, but can be as harmless as a bird in the yard. The dog's barking annoys everyone within earshot. If you live close to other houses, the barking may even get someone to call complain to the authorities.

You can stop the barking by having your dog wear an anti-bark collar when he's outside. Many dogs won't even run along the fence when they can't bark. Even if they do run back and forth, they'll do it quietly.

Another way to handle the barker-runner is to arrange the area so the dog can't see anything to bark at outside the fence. The most attractive way to do this is to plant bushes on the outside of the fence. If this is not practical, you could attach some sort of solid barrier to the outside of the fence to block the dog's view. Home improvement stores sell materials for this purpose; people put them on swimming pool fences so that they can go skinny-dipping in private. Don't use those aluminum strips that are woven into chain-link fences; many dogs will pull them out.

I'm thinking about having a fence installed.

Good idea. If it is within your budget and can be arranged on your premises, a fence will make dog owning much easier for you. If you're having a fence installed, you have the opportunity to plan it so that it will be convenient to use in all weather.

If possible, put the fenced enclosure adjacent to the house so you can just open the door to let Princie out. If you can't do this, you'll just have to walk him out to his yard.

If you live in the city, check the building codes. Some municipalities don't allow fences at all. Some allow only certain types of fences. Check before you start; avoid problems with the local government.

Pick the best fence that your budget can handle. Chain link is the industry standard for dog enclosures. Chain link fences for dogs are usually four feet high and made of eleven-gauge wire. You can buy more costly fence made of nine-gauge wire and six feet high, but in most cases this is an unnecessary expense.

Standard chain link dog fencing is made with two-inch openings between the wires, more expensive fencing is made with one-inch openings. The bigger the openings, the more easily the fence can be climbed, which may be an issue if your dog is a potential climber.

Woven wire fencing that is made for farm animals is less expensive than chain link, and is satisfactory if the fence is installed with enough line posts to keep it rigid. Line posts for woven wire fence should be a maximum of ten or 12 feet apart, to prevent an active dog from stretching the fence enough to crawl under it.

If your dog's yard will adjoin your neighbors' yard, consider installing a solid fence such as a wooden stockade between the two yards. This will keep your dog from seeing (and barking at) the neighbors.

How big should I make my dog's yard? This depends on how much space you have in your yard, and, to some extent, the size of your dog. A Chihuahua will be content in a 12-foot square; a Great Dane would enjoy half an acre. Remember, you'll have to clean up the yard. Don't make it too big.

What about an Invisible Fence?

Invisible Fence is actually a brand name for this type of fence. Other manufacturers make similar equipment. If you've never used an invisible fence, this system consists of an electrified buried wire around the perimeter of an area and a receiver collar worn by the dog. The collar gives the dog a little shock if it approaches the boundary. The dog must be trained to avoid crossing the boundary, which is easily done. The fence comes with little flags to mark the area and an instruction video to show you how to train your dog to respond correctly.

Consider the advantages and disadvantages to an invisible fence before you decide to have one installed:

> Since the fence is invisible, it is acceptable where a wire fence is not permitted or is considered to be unsightly.

> A dog cannot dig under, jump over, or squeeze through the force field of an invisible fence.

> It is less expensive to enclose a large area with an invisible fence than it is to use a wire fence.

> Some bold dogs will accept the shock and run through the fence. Some dogs will stay behind an invisible fence only until something really attractive is on the other side to lure them out. Some dogs have a coat thick enough to prevent the shock from reaching their skin. These dogs must have a patch of hair clipped off their necks to allow them to feel the shock.

> An invisible fence is not a barrier to a dog that is not wearing a receiver collar. Any stray dog can come into your yard and harm the dog that is confined there.

Can I confine my dog on a chain?

No dog should live on a chain. No dog should be confined chained to a doghouse or a garage for hours at a time. No dog should be on a chain so short that it has to step in its own waste. This doesn't mean that a chain cannot be used properly to control your dog when it's outside.

With a correct chain setup, you can allow your dog appropriate time outdoors for elimination and for limited exercise. You can arrange the chain so that you don't have to go very far outside in bad weather. You can make one of the hardest parts of dog ownership—taking the dog outside—easy.

What kind of a chain should I use?

First, you need the correct chain. Of course, the size of the chain depends on the size of your dog. Most brands of dog chains are available in three or four weights. If you have a St. Bernard, you'll need the heaviest, strongest dog chain available. If you have a Pomeranian, buy the lightest chain they have. It is never advisable to use a rope for tying out your dog. You'd be surprised at what an innocent little dog can chew through.

Dog chains usually come in 10, 15, 20, and occasionally

25-foot lengths. The length you'll choose depends on the space your dog will be allowed to occupy and where you will install the chain. Before you buy a chain, go outside and step off the area where Princie will be confined. The usual length of a lady's step is two feet, a man's step about three feet. Step alongside a yardstick to measure the length of your own stride.

Many commercial dog chains are made of twisted figure-eight wire links. These chains come with a tongue-type snap on each end, the snap on one end for the dog's collar and the other snap to attach to a stationary object.

Chains made of twisted wire links with tongue snaps on both ends are the least expensive of the chains made for dogs. Chains of this type are perfectly satisfactory if used correctly, but they have two drawbacks: first, the links are made of wire and wear out before welded links. If you use a twisted-wire link chain, check the links every month or so to be sure that the wire isn't getting so thin that it will break. Be sure to examine the links near the snap where the chains seem to wear first. If you buy the right size wire-link chain for your dog, you might have to replace it only every year or so, maybe even less often.

The other problem with those inexpensive chains is that the tongue snaps can be very rigid and hard to open. The snaps have to stay closed (or the dog will escape) so they are made of inflexible steel. This need not be a problem; you can attach your dog to its chain with an additional snap.

Check the snaps on your chain for wear. Almost all snaps are made of two parts: a snap on one end that fits into a swivel on the other end. The bottom part of the snap that goes through the swivel is subject can wear thin enough to come out of the swivel when your dog pulls on the chain.

Dog chains made of welded steel links are available for medium and larger dogs. These chains will cost nearly twice as much as the chains made of twisted wire links, but they still are not prohibitively expensive. Chains made of welded links are not as subject to wear and will last for many years. An added attraction of the welded-link chains is that they usually are supplied with much better snaps.

Cable tie-outs to use instead of chains are available for really big dogs. These are made of twisted steel strands, sometimes with a plastic coating. Cables are very strong, but so are welded wire chains. Cables are significantly less flexible than chains; chains are the better choice for most uses.

Attaching your dog's chain to the house.

In some cases, all you have to do is to snap one end of the chain around a stationary object such as a porch railing, and the other end on your dog. This is satisfactory for very small dogs, but for larger dogs, you'll need to attach the chain more securely.

Overhead cable dog run

An overhead cable is a time-tested satisfactory way of allowing your chained dog to have a lot of freedom outdoors. A steel cable is stretched tight between two sturdy objects at a height of six feet or more. A pulley is usually put on the chain before it is installed. The dog's chain is snapped to the pulley; the dog can run up and down the length of the overhead cable.

With an overhead cable run, you'll need only a 10-foot chain of a weight suitable to the size of your dog. The dog is not confined to the length of the chain, since the chain slides along the entire length of the cable.

It's best to buy a strong commercial cable made for a dog

run, and to install the cable with a turnbuckle at one or both ends. When the cable loosens, which it will eventually, the slack can be taken out of it with the turnbuckle.

Tree trolley.

If there is a sturdy tree (or post) in a convenient spot in your yard, you can use this as an anchor for your dog chain. Snap one end of the chain around the tree in a loop bigger than the diameter of the trunk. That way, the chain loop can slide freely around the tree and give your dog more freedom. If you are anchoring your dog chain to a live tree, use a length of garden hose (or old vacuum cleaner hose, or anything similar) on the part of the chain that encircles the tree. This prevents the chain from damaging the bark.

Tie-out stake.

I'm sure you've seen those corkscrew metal stakes, about 16 inches long, with a handle and a swivel on one end. The handle is used to screw the stake into the ground, the swivel to attach the dog's chain. The stake should be screwed entirely into the ground with only the swivel and handle above ground.

Don't buy a straight tie-out stake unless Princie weighs less than 15 pounds; they are too easy for a dog to pull out of the ground. A straight tie-out stake is just a metal rod with a plate and a swivel at the top. The stake is hammered into the ground to the level of the plate. It is not a very strong device.

The advantage of a tie-out stake is that it is inexpensive, easy to install, and easy to move. The disadvantage is that a strong dog can pull these stakes, even the corkscrew ones, out of the ground. A stake that seems sturdy in dry weather can be pulled out easily when the ground is soft after a rain. If you have even a medium-sized dog, a tie-out stake is not a really good idea. You may see Princie running down the street, dragging his chain and stake.

If possible, install the chain where you can reach the dog's end from the door of your house. That way, you don't have to go out in bad weather to put your dog safely on his chain. You just grab the chain, snap it on the dog's collar and release him.

Install your chain in a location free of objects that can entangle the dog. If Princie gets tangled in bushes, you'll have to go out to release him and free the chain, which is a nuisance in the dark or in bad weather.

If you have two dogs and want to use chains for both of them, be sure that the dogs cannot contact each other and become tangled together. Never put two dogs on a single overhead cable. This sounds obvious, but humane officers have been called to rescue entangled dogs. Sometimes one or both of the dogs are not still alive. Warning: A dog on a chain is not protected from other dogs that may come into your yard. Never leave your dog tied outside when you are away.

If you have difficulty with the snap that came attached to your dog's chain, go to any hardware store, look at their display of all sorts and sizes of snaps, try them out, and pick out one that is easy for you to use. No, you don't have to take off the old snap; just clip the old snap onto the eye of the new one.

Short lead-out chain.

If you must install your tie-out chain where you can't reach it from the house, you'll have to lead your dog to the chain every time you tie it outside. Unless you really trust your dog to obey, you'll have to use some sort of leash for this purpose.

Buy a short, four-foot chain leash. Keep this short chain in the house. When you are ready to tie Princie outside, attach one end of the short chain to his collar and use this little chain to lead him to the longer tie-out chain. No need to take the short chain off the dog's collar; just snap the long chain onto the ring that holds the hand loop of the short chain leash.

If you prefer to have a snap on each end of your lead-out chain, buy a double-ended snap or an open-ring snap and put it on the ring at the end of the short chain leash. You can take off the hand loop, or just leave it in place for your convenience.

If you are going to use a lead-out chain, remember to include its length in the total chain required to restrain your dog in the area.

If you live in a cold climate, you might want to use a short lead-out chain even if your long chain is close to the door. That way, the snaps on your short chain won't be frozen because you keep it in the house. If you find that you can't get your dog off its chain because the end snap is frozen, you'll have to take off a mitten and hold the snap in your warm hand for a few seconds.

What kind of a collar should I use to tie my dog outside?

Unless you have a small docile dog, the collar that you use to walk your dog on a leash is not the same as the collar you will use to chain it outside. For tying your dog outside, use a plain buckle collar, either flat or round, leather or fabric, but not a choke collar, a choke chain, or any collar that can slip over the dog's head. If your dog gets entangled with anything while wearing a choke collar, it could be strangled. And many dogs are extremely clever at backing out of or scratching off any collar that loosens when there is no tension on the chain or leash.

The size and thickness of the collar must be such that it will restrain your dog if it decides to pull against it. Remember that a leather collar will stretch when it gets wet; a nylon collar will not.

Don't use a harness to tie your dog on a chain. Very few harnesses are positively escape-proof. You might come to get your dog and find the harness and chain on the ground and Princie in the neighbor's yard.

What should I do about my dog's waste in the yard?

Clean up after your dog regularly. It is an unfortunate fact of dog ownership that the waste produced by your dog must be removed. Daily cleanup is an absolute necessity if you confine your dog on a chain in a relatively small area. If you have a large fenced yard for your dog, you probably can get away with cleaning up dog waste on alternate days in very cold weather.

There are important reasons other than the appearance and odor for promptly removing fecal material from your yard. Dog waste attracts insects that will fly into your house every time you open the door. If your dog has internal parasites (worms), the parasite eggs will develop in the waste and will re-infect your dog. Feces can be the source of several other bacterial and viral diseases.

Don't hire the neighbor's child to pick up your dog's waste in the yard unless you talk to the parents first. Hire a child only if he or she is old enough and responsible enough to do the job properly.

We never like to think about this, but many dogs will eat stools. This is called coprophagia, and is a learned behavior. Prevent and avoid this problem: pick up dog waste promptly.

Use the right equipment to remove your dog's waste. Pooper Scoopers often are sold at the same place you bought your other dog equipment. These usually consist of two pieces: a sort of a shovel, and a sort of a rake. Rake the dog droppings onto the shovel, then dump the droppings into whatever container you use for disposal. If you'd rather use pickup bags for dog droppings, put your hand inside the bag, pick up the droppings with your bag-covered hand, then turn the bag inside-out so that the droppings are inside, nice and neat. If you want to use this method and have a small dog (with small droppings), you can use the cheapest plastic sandwich bags just as well as those made especially for dog waste.

Depending on the final disposal of the droppings, you can pick them up with several pieces of paper towel, or even a piece of newspaper. If you pick up dog droppings with a piece of paper, you must have a disposal method that will allow you to include the paper as well as the waste.

If you have difficulty cleaning up after your dog or disposing of its solid waste, consider employing a professional service that will do this for you. These services come to your yard once or twice a week, pick up the droppings, and take the waste away for disposal. Search under "Pet Waste Removal" in the Yellow Pages or online. If professional waste removal services are too costly or are not available in your area, you might be able to hire a high school student for twice-weekly cleanup. A phone call to the nearest high school might be the way to locate a student who wants to earn a little extra money.

What to do with all those droppings?

It's tempting just to put them in the trash. Many municipalities that have regular trash pickups specify "no animal waste."

I'm not suggesting that you break rules, but unless you have a couple of large dogs, you probably can wrap the droppings in lots of newspapers and get away with placing them in your regular trash. Be sure that the droppings are wrapped securely and can't come undone when the trash is dumped.

Consider taking the dog droppings inside and flushing them down the toilet. This works very well unless you have a lot of waste for disposal, or if you try to flush down a big wad of waste and paper, or even a large amount of waste in a plastic removal bag. If you do, keep your plunger handy. The stuff won't go down.

If you happen to live in a rural area or have a property with an appropriate remote location, you could use a covered container (such as a small garbage can) for the waste. Empty it, far away from the house, every few days. Sprinkle hydrated lime on the droppings in the covered container and more lime on the dumped pile.

Hydrated lime is a white powder that is used to reduce the acidity of the floors of horse and cattle stalls. Lime is sold in 50-pound bags at feed stores; one bag will last for years. Keep the bag of lime in the garage and use an empty dog food can to scoop out what you need.

Chapter 4
Controlling Your Dog on the Street

When the door is closed, Princie is a perfect gentleman. But just reach for the knob—Princie sees his way to freedom. He gets excited, tries to push out of the door, refuses to hold still for you to attach his leash, and generally makes it a struggle to even take him out in the yard for elimination or exercise.

When you finally manage to get the leash on and the door open, Princie yanks you out and goes his merry way, ignoring you at the end of his leash. All those new smells. It's no fun to have a dog pull you up and down the street. It's particularly no fun when the weather is bad and the sidewalks are slippery. It's even less fun when the neighbor's dog runs out and Princie tries to dislocate your arm to get to it. And if he does manage to escape your control, Princie can cause a dogfight, can scamper out of sight, can even be hit by a passing car.

One of the major benefits and major pleasures of dog ownership is having a companion to take for walks. Your doctor will tell you that walking is one of the best ways to stay fit and active. Having a dog will ensure that you get out and get that exercise.

The best arrangement for you and your dog is to have both

forms of outdoor activity: outside in a fenced yard (or on a chain) for elimination, and leash walking for exercise. When you have both options, you don't have to get dressed to take your dog out in bad weather or in the dark; he can go out in the yard without you. When it's time for exercise, put the leash on your dog and go for a hike.

My dog is too strong. He drags me wherever he wants to go.

It isn't any fun to walk with a dog that is hard to control. It certainly isn't safe to walk an out-of-control dog in wet or slippery conditions or near traffic. Eliminate the chance that your dog will pull you off your feet or force you to let go of the leash. Don't get yanked from tree to tree or dread the sight of another dog.

Use the right equipment. No matter if your dog is big, strong, and determined, no matter if you are small and cautious, you don't have to have your arm pulled out when you take it for a walk.

Some of the equipment that will allow you to control your dog might seem unkind to use, but consider the alternate: you may not be able to walk your dog at all if it puts you in danger. If the dog is in control, it is not safe for you, and it is not safe for your dog.

What kind of a collar should I use for walking my dog?

If you have a small docile dog, use anything convenient to walk it on a leash. But if you have even a medium-sized active and determined dog, the collar that you use to tie it out on its chain is not appropriate for walking it on the street. Your tie-out collar should be a plain buckle type, and not one that causes any discomfort to the dog if it pulls. To walk a strong dog safely and comfortably, you need a device that makes it uncomfortable for the dog to try to take control.

"Choke" collars.

Any type of collar that can tighten like a noose on a dog's neck is a "choke" collar. This includes the so-called limited-choke or martingale collars, which only tighten part of the way. Chain choke collars are the most common, but choke collars are also made of leather or nylon.

You've probably discovered that any choke collar, chain, leather, or fabric, is next to useless on a strong, determined dog. A big dog's neck is much stronger and more muscular than is a person's neck. A yank that would strangle a person is hardly noticed by an active dog. Also, most dogs are perfectly willing to pull hard enough on a choke collar to actually gag and make funny noises while pulling. Even though these collars are used by obedience trainers and in the show ring, they won't restrain your big strong dog enough to make you comfortable or safe while walking it.

"The pinch" collar.

Also called a "prong" collar or a "force" collar, pinch collars have small inward projections that prick the dog's neck when the leash is tightened. This sounds more unkind than it actually is, since the prongs are not sharp. However, a sharp jerk on the leash is usually enough to stop a very determined dog. Very few dogs will ignore the pressure of a pinch collar.

Most pinch collars are made of metal links that fit together, connected by a chain to which the leash is fastened. Some pinch collars are made of plastic links and a chain. To work properly, a pinch collar be fitted correctly to the dog that is wearing it. The most common mistake is to adjust the collar too large. If the collar can be slipped over the dog's head without unfastening it, the person on the end of the leash can't control the dog with only slight pressure. Pinch collars are easy to adjust by removing the extra links.

There is nothing cruel about the pinch collar when fitted and used correctly. You may find a pinch collar to be the answer to your dog-walking problems.

The head collar.

Also called a head halter, these control devices resemble the halters used on livestock. The principle is the same: if you have control of the head, you have control of the body too.

Several brands of head collars are on the market. Look for Halti, Gentle Leader, or similar brands in pet stores. Head collars are made only for medium and large dogs, since smaller dogs don't require that much restraint. Check the package for the correct size for your breed of dog. If you have any doubts as to the fit, take your dog to a pet store that has helpful clerks.

Head collars are really good restraint devices for walking even the strongest dog. No pulling, no yanking, you are always in control. But head collars have a couple of drawbacks. Your dog will have to get used to the feeling of something around his muzzle. At first, the dog will probably paw at the head collar or try to scratch it off. Teach your dog to wear its head collar by putting it on, attaching the leash to the ring at the bottom of the dog's jaw, and just start walking, coaxing "Come, Princie, come." Keep walking. Don't let Princie stop to scratch at the collar. You might want to give him a little treat occasionally to keep him moving on his own. A dog wearing a head collar has no choice but to follow his leader.

You also can't leave the head collar on your dog when you are not walking it, because the dog will certainly scratch it off, chew it up, or lose it. This means that the device must be buckled on your dog every time you take it out on a leash. This is not at all hard to do unless Princie resists vigorously. If he does, try restraining him with a temporary noose leash and offering him some treats when you put on the head collar.

The anti-pull harness.

Don't confuse an anti-pull harness with regular harnesses. A regular harness is an absolute invitation for a dog to pull on the leash, and not suitable for anything but a Chihuahua-sized dog.

An anti-pull harness restricts the movement of the dog's front legs so that it can't put pressure on the leash. When the leash is slack, the dog has full freedom; when the leash is tight, it is restrained.

The head collar is probably the best device for walking strong dogs. The pinch collar is a close second, and may be better if you have a lot of trouble getting a head collar on your dog. The anti-pull harness has the advantage of appearing to be more humane, but the disadvantage of being tiresome to put on your dog every time you go for a walk.

What is the best kind of leash? How long should my leash be?

Any leash that is strong enough to hold your dog is just fine for walking it on the street. Use a leash of plain flat or round leather, fabric, or nylon. Never use a chain leash to walk your dog. A dog pulling on a chain leash will hurt your hands if you hold the leash by any part except the hand loop. If you can't grab the leash anyplace except the end, you'll find it very awkward to keep your dog under control.

For medium and large dogs, select a sturdy leash that is a half or three-quarters inch wide. For small dogs, you may prefer a narrower leash.

Dog leashes usually are supplied in four, six, and ten-foot lengths. You'll find the four-foot ones are entirely too short to allow Princie any freedom. Trainers usually recommend the six-foot leashes. You can buy really long (15 or 20-foot) leashes, but you may find these too long to be convenient. Remember, a dog that has a 20-foot run before it hits the end of the leash can give you quite a jolt.

Retractable leashes consist of a plastic housing with a handhold, inside of which is a spring-loaded leash. There is no slack in these leashes; the leash lengthens and shortens as the dog pulls. The diameter of retractable leashes makes them suitable only for small dogs.

Before you buy any leash, examine the snap on the end. Is it sturdy? Is it easy to open and close? If it isn't, select another leash.

How do I clean up after my dog on street?

If you live in the city, it is likely that municipal rules require that you remove your dog's waste from the area. Even if there are no such rules, it is only polite to remove Princie's droppings from other people's property. A little dog urine is not harmful to most bushes, but many people become irate if Princie lifts his leg on their petunias. It's best to keep your dog away from areas where it is not welcome, and this includes your neighbor's lawn.

You can buy plastic bags made for picking up dog droppings. Use these bags, or use cheaper plastic sandwich bags, especially if Princie is a small dog and has small droppings. Put your hand inside the bag, pick up the dropping, then turn the bag inside-out so the droppings are neatly inside. The big problem is what to do with the plastic-enclosed waste after you pick it up. Carry a paper bag (maybe two paper bags, one inside the other), drop the waste inside, and dump the (well-wrapped) paper bag in the trash when you get home.

What should I do if we meet another dog?

Any loose dog can be a real hazard. The most aggressive dog is the one that runs out from its own property when you and Princie walk past. This dog feels that it is protecting its home and it is likely to bite. Before you walk your dog in a new area, consider driving the route or walking alone to check on the presence of loose dogs. In most municipalities, it is against local rules to allow a dog to run loose. If you spot a loose dog, consider reporting it to the authorities. You don't have to have the name of the owner, just the street name and the house number. In almost all cases, reports to police about loose dogs are anonymous.

Many loose dogs will be friendly or only curious. Don't wait to see if the loose dog is aggressive. Take precautions right away.

> Head in the other direction as soon as you see a loose dog. Don't run. Watch to see if the dog follows.

> If the dog follows, stop and yell, "Get out of here."

> Don't pick up Princie even if he is very small. If the loose dog is aggressive, it may jump on you, knock you down and injure you. Both you and your dog may be bitten.

> Carry a weapon to protect yourself. A big black cane-umbrella is the best protection you can carry easily. Closed, you can use it as a cane for walking. When a loose dog approaches, open the umbrella (practice getting it open quickly at home) and shove it point first into the dog's face while yelling at the top of your lungs. Almost every dog will back off.

> Leave the area as fast as you can without running. Watch your back. Keep the umbrella open until you are sure the loose dog is gone.

If you meet another dog walker with a dog on a leash, just ask the owner to keep the dog away from yours. Unless you know the person and the dog, it isn't a good idea even to let the dogs sniff noses. If you meet a dog walker who walks his dog off-leash, ask him to keep the dog away from yours. Hopefully, he will be courteous and comply. If he doesn't, you'll have to treat the loose dog like one that has no owner nearby.

Where can I buy all the equipment used in this chapter?

Collars, leashes, cables, chains, harnesses, head collars and all the rest of the equipment are commonly available locally. Hardware stores, feed stores, pet stores, and pet food sections in grocery stores are ready sources. If you prefer to buy by mail, the appendix has a number of catalog sources. You can even buy dog equipment on the internet; just access "dog supplies." If you live near a large, national-chain pet store, this is a good place to get what you need. These stores usually welcome shoppers and their dogs. Take Princie along and get his equipment fitted to him by a knowledgeable salesperson.

Chapter 5
When to Seek Professional Help for Your Dog

"My dog doesn't listen to a thing I say. I can't make it mind me at all. Should I take it to obedience school? Would it be easier to have someone else train it? Would that be too expensive?

Dog training classes are the most available and the least expensive help you can get in shaping your dog's behavior. These classes should be called "owner training classes." You are the one who will see how a dog learns and how to use this knowledge to make your dog an agreeable and obedient companion. You might enjoy training classes enough to participate in advanced training.

Training classes and obedience trials have been around a long time. Formal obedience training and trials originated in Germany and other parts of Europe early in the twentieth century. The Germans had a reputation for being strict disciplinarians; most of the dogs being trained were shepherds and Dobermans. Persuasion and food rewards were foreign concepts to these early trainers. The dogs obeyed or they suffered the consequences.

The sport of dog obedience training came to the United

States in 1934. Blanche Saunders, a Standard Poodle breeder, heard about European training and trials, went to observe them in action. She returned to the United States and started dog training classes. Within ten years, the American Kennel Club had established obedience trials throughout the United States.

In 1946, Saunders authored, *Training You to Train Your Dog*, a book long considered to be the bible of the sport. Although her methods might be considered harsh by today's standards, the book contains valuable information about a dog's mind and appropriate suggestions to help an owner make his dog an agreeable companion.

Should I take my dog to a training class?

Absolutely yes, if you possibly can. Training classes can be the most valuable source of professional help that you can get to shape your dog's behavior.

Most people, including most seniors, are not a bit interested in training their dogs to obedience trial standards. Fortunately, many trainers recognize this. The majority of today's trainers and training classes stress home behavior, not competitive skills.

In a properly run training class, you will learn the meaning of positive and negative reinforcement and how to use these methods. You will gain knowledge that you will apply with great effect to every dog you own for the rest of your life.

Consider hiring a private trainer only if your dog has behavior issues that you have been unable to resolve and that you find difficult or impossible to live with. Private trainers may come to your house only once as a consultant, or several times to give you instructions and to check up on your progress.

Since these private-trainer sessions involve the trainer's time, expertise, and travel, they are likely to be quite expensive. Some trainers are absolutely worth the money; their suggestions will get you well on your way to solving your dog problems. Other trainers will spend their time and your money and not produce any lasting improvement in your problems. If you decide to try a private trainer, you must select the kind of trainer that will be of the greatest benefit to you and your dog.

Ask for referrals from obedience class trainers. Tell these trainers about your difficulty in attending their classes. They will understand. Some of these trainers do in-home training as well as instruct classes.

Have very specific goals in mind. For example, "my dog won't let me put his leash on." Or "my dog wants to attack everyone he sees passing the house." Discuss these problems with the trainer before you agree to a home visit. Ask if the trainer has had experience with your type of problem and if she thinks she can offer a solution.

Some trainers will keep dogs at their own facilities for a specific length of time for training. Some even take young dogs into their own homes for housebreaking. These services will be costly, as they include boarding as well as training.

How can I find the right trainer or the right training class?

The best way to find good dog trainers and training classes is to ask for recommendations from your friends, your veterinarian, or from the local humane society. These people will recommend only trainers about whom they hear good things. Some veterinarians and humane societies sponsor their own training classes, which are likely to be well run and effective.

The yellow pages of your telephone book have many listings for trainers. Look under "kennels" or "pet training." If you live in a major metropolitan area, there will be several pages of these advertisements. If you live in a suburban or rural area, there will be only a page or so of these listings. Don't believe everything the ads say; anyone can write an ad but only a skilled and experienced trainer can help you with your dog. If you decide to choose a class or a trainer from the telephone book, ask for referrals from people who have used their services.

Question your friends who have used trainers or have taken their dogs to training classes. If they were not satisfied with the results, better look for a different trainer.

How can I tell if a trainer is any good?

Companion dog training has become a profession. At present, there is no standard of experience or expertise required for a person to be a professional dog trainer. The National Association of Pet Dog Trainers is an organization that stresses the education of its members in modern, effective, and humane methods of training dogs and owners. Members of this association are likely to be competent, but non-members with a great deal of experience are also likely to be effective trainers.

Many people are dog trainers on a full-time or part time basis. Some own kennels, raise and show dogs, or board and groom dogs and have expanded their businesses to include dog training. Some of these trainers have had years of experience with hundreds of dogs; some have just trained their own dogs and decide that it would be enjoyable and profitable to expand their businesses and train other people's dogs. It can be difficult to tell if these people are effective trainers. Ask for referrals from owners whom the trainers have helped. Telephone the referrals and question them about the problems they had with their dogs. You will get a realistic idea of the help these trainers can offer.

If at all possible, observe trainers at work. Before you enroll your dog, attend a couple of obedience classes as a spectator. Do you like the trainers' methods? Do the dogs seem to be learning? Do the dogs seem fearful or are they happy? Are the trainers kind and pleasant, or do they shout and bully owners or dogs?

Do the trainers stress things that your dog needs to learn? Are they obedience-trial oriented or home behavior oriented? Is there any danger from aggressive dogs to other dogs in the class, or are appropriate measures taken to keep those dogs apart?

Does the trainer use and recommend appropriate equipment? Since all class members are not alike, does the trainer use equipment designed to control dogs of different sizes and temperaments? Does the trainer furnish or tell you where to buy effective training collars and leads? Does he or she show you how to fit the equipment to your dog?

Beware of the trainer who uses very harsh methods. There is no place in training for beating, hitting, or choking a dog. Remember, "hitting" doesn't include a mild tap on the hindquarters to remind a dog to sit. "Choking" doesn't include a little jerk of the leash to reinforce come. There is one exception to the rule of no harsh methods: if someone gets careless and one dog attacks another, any method is entirely acceptable to break up the combatants.

Just as you should beware of trainers who use brutal methods, you should be suspicious of those who advocate too-lax methods. Modern "humane" training tends toward rewarding (usually with food) correct behavior and ignoring bad behavior, on the theory that the lack of reward will cause a dog to quit its undesirable actions. "Work to earn reward" of food or praise is effective only if the food or praise is more interesting to the dog than doing as it pleases. Just as with children, what works for one dog may be ignored by another. Good trainers know the difference, but many trainers don't. These continue to practice very mild methods ineffectively on very tough dogs. Observe the results.

Beware of trainers that tell you always to have your pockets full of food. Bribes are useful to teach and to reinforce a favorable behavior, but you should be shown how and when to phase out the tidbits. A trained dog should obey even when you don't offer it food.

Think twice about a training method that requires you always to have some sort of specialized equipment in hand. This pertains particularly to "clicker" training. The trainer uses the noise of a mechanical clicker to indicate approval and to reinforce good behavior. Personally, I have enough trouble keeping track of my eyeglasses, let alone a mechanical device. Instead of the noise of a clicker, you can say: "yes!" or "good!" or even "click!" It will work just the same and you won't have to worry if you leave the clicker in another pocket.

I have special needs. Can a professional trainer help?

Some professional trainers can help while some certainly cannot. The trainer who specializes in training for obedience trial competition won't have any knowledge or interest in helping a senior owner who uses a cane. The sight-impaired owner needs the help of a trainer who understands his problems. Ask at the local senior center if they know any trainers that specialize in helping owners with handicaps. Before you hire a professional trainer, question him or her about previous experiences.

We once trained a Labrador retriever for a paraplegic man who loved to hunt ducks. He hunted from an all-terrain vehicle. His dog was a good natural retriever, but she wouldn't ride with him in the vehicle, wouldn't wait until he sent her for a downed bird, and wouldn't jump into the all-terrain vehicle to bring the bird to him.

We didn't have an ATV, so first we taught the dog to jump into a lawn cart attached behind a riding mower. Then we taught her to ride in the cart when it was in motion. Next we taught her to stay in the cart while we threw a dummy bird, and to jump out to fetch the dummy only on command. The rest was easy—the dog already knew how to jump into the cart, so she brought the "bird" with her. The dog considered the all-terrain vehicle to be the same as a lawn cart, and the owner was delighted.

This is an example of incremental training. A complex task is broken up into several small steps that are trained in sequence. Dogs can learn very difficult behaviors by the use of this method.

Are there other sources of professional help for my dog's behavior problems?

Colleges of Veterinary Medicine often have staff veterinarians who specialize in behavior problems. Some veterinary practices offer behavior consultation. You can locate veterinary behaviorists by asking your own veterinarian or your local Academy of Veterinary Medicine.

These specialized practices are usually found only in large metropolitan areas. Veterinarians in these practices often prescribe drugs as well as conditioning to help change dogs' behavior. Generally only the most severe cases are treated by veterinary behaviorists, as the consultations and drug purchases are likely to be immensely expensive and time consuming.

You might consider reading library books or renting videos to help you improve your dog's behavior. "Courses" on the Internet may be costly and may not relate to your special problems. Beware of courses that promise to teach you "training secrets" for a fee. Beware of trainers with "guarantees," or "secret methods." There are no secrets in dog training.

A trainer is only worth the time and money if he or she teaches you how to solve your dog problems. Remember, the trainer won't be around all the time.

Part II: Giving Your Dog the Best Care

Chapter 6
Exercising Your Dog

Dogs are like humans; youngsters of both species run and play. Mature animals exercise toward a goal. There is a great deal of difference between the exercise an animal enjoys and the exercise that it actually needs.

Dogs and all members of the canine family are essentially meat-eaters. What is the main activity of wild canines? Hunting for food, of course. If they don't hunt successfully, they don't eat. When game is scarce, wild dogs may exercise to exhaustion just to obtain a meal. When game is plentiful, wild dogs catch and eat their prey, then spend the remainder of their time in "leisure" activities. Pups may play with one another; adults sometimes seek mates and defend their territories from other canines. Except for these activities, resting and sleeping are the main leisure activities of wild dogs with full stomachs. Wolves that are kept in captivity and are given regular meals seldom find it necessary to exercise at all.

The first domestic dogs had functions to fulfill. Hounds and bird dogs helped obtain food that they shared with their humans. When they were not hunting, these dogs curled up in their kennels. Guard dogs were (and are) supposed to stay home. Guards are not performing their function if they are away from the areas they are supposed to protect.

Herding dogs were and still are probably the most active canines, since they must control large numbers of other animals. Even herding dogs go lie down in the shade when their charges are under control. We never consider that dogs that guide the blind are deprived of exercise, yet these animals get exactly as much exercise and activity as do their owners.

How important is the age of my dog to the exercise it wants?

The age of your dog is more important than its size or breed in determining the amount of exercise that it would like. Puppies want to play and explore. This is a characteristic of young animals that are curious and are just learning about the world. Since a dog can be considered to be a puppy from birth to about 18 months of age, it is the younger dogs that want to be the most active. Most dogs grow out of puppy behavior at two or three years old. Some dogs seem to be puppies in their behavior throughout most of their lives.

It is an old wives' tale that the reason that your young dog chews objects in the house is because it doesn't get enough exercise. Don't believe it. Even if you exercise your puppy to exhaustion, it will nap for a while and then it will look for something new to play with or explore.

What about my dog's size?

Little dogs are just as rowdy, just as active, and just as playful as big dogs. Rowdy little dogs just aren't as disturbing as rowdy larger ones, merely because of their size.

The bigger the dog, the longer its stride. A Pekinese takes

four or five times the number of steps walking a mile than does a Great Dane. Tiny dogs may be tired out in short walks, big ones can walk many miles.

Its size determines the amount of exercise a dog can get in a small area. Throwing a ball in your living room is appropriate for your fox terrier, but throwing a ball in your living room for your shepherd isn't a good idea unless you put all breakable items away before you begin.

Do some breeds need more exercise?

The breed of your dog not nearly as important as is its age and size in determining the amount of exercise and entertainment that it wants. Even though some breeds were developed for hunting, herding, or even racing, adult members of these breeds are usually willing to lead relatively sedentary lives.

Belle, my family's greyhound, was tall, slim, long-legged, and young. Yet my childhood memory of Belle is that she spent most of her 15 years asleep under the piano. Spike, the little fox terrier, was always into everything. It's the inherited temperament of each individual, along with its age, not its breed, that determines the amount of activity a dog desires.

It certainly seems that a dog's inherited behavior is important in determining the amount of entertainment it seeks. There is little question that some breeds use their brains in different ways than other breeds. For example, my Border collie's ancestors had to take complicated directions from their masters when they handled flocks of sheep. The ancestors of Belle the greyhound were required only to run as fast as they could. When Belle wasn't running, she was happy to sleep. The Border collie seems to be in constant motion.

Your dog's routine is very important.

Try to give your young or middle-aged dog 15 to 30 minutes of exercise, playtime, or activity once or twice a day. You will benefit as much as your dog when both of you exercise regularly.

If your dog spends any significant part of its time in its Safe Place, be sure to give it regular, frequent periods of activity. The dog that is confined for some of the time needs at least three or four 15-minute playtimes a day. The dog that spends its leisure time lying at your feet will be satisfied with less activity.

Your senior dog doesn't want or need as much activity as a young or middle-aged animal. There is no way to define a "senior" dog, any more than there is a way to define a "senior" person while some dogs are very spry at 12 years of age, some are quite inactive. In general, it is the larger (and the overweight) dogs that seem to age the fastest. A giant breed such as a Saint Bernard may be a senior at seven or eight years of age; a fox terrier still acts young at ten or 12.

The kind of exercise is also important.

Your dog will get more exercise in 15 minutes of chasing a ball than in an hour of walking on a leash. Of course, you won't be exercising much when you just throw the ball. A good routine for both of you would be to plan a daily walk and a daily "fetch" time. You can vary this schedule according to your preference and the weather: a morning and an afternoon walk in good weather and two "fetch" or playtimes when it's raining.

Will my dog get fat without exercise?

Only one thing makes a normal human or a normal dog fat:

consuming more calories than its body uses. Yes, exercise uses calories, but it takes a lot of exercise to burn only a little fat. You must be your dog's conscience: feed your dog only enough to keep it at a healthy weight. Ignore it if it begs for more.

I'm getting a new dog.

If you are choosing another dog, consider its size and age in relation to the amount of activity you are able to give it. You might prefer a small or medium-sized dog that can get enough exercise in a relatively small area or from a relatively short walk.

A puppy is seldom a good choice. Many, many full-grown dogs of every breed, type and size are looking for homes. Chose an adult dog. That way, you won't have to live through its troublesome puppy stages.

How can I provide exercise and entertainment for my dog?

Take your dog with you. Whenever possible, take your dog along when you visit family and friends. Be sure that Rover will be welcome and well behaved in someone else's house before you go.

Arrange a play date for your dog. Invite a friend with a compatible dog. Rover will love to run and play in the yard, or even in the house, with another dog. If your dog loves children, perhaps your grandchildren would like a visit to play with Rover.

Take a hike. Walking is a wonderful exercise for you as well as for your dog. Establish a routine: a thirty-minute walk every afternoon, a 15-minute walk twice a day, or an hour's stroll when the weather permits. Both you and your dog will feel better, will have more pep, and will look forward to your little outings.

Play "fetch" in the yard or in the house. Many dogs like to chase things and play "fetch," even though they might not deliver their toys to their owners' hands. All you need are a couple of tennis balls to throw alternately. This game is much better played in the yard than in the house, especially if you have a sizeable dog and value your china lamps. If your dog has no inclination to chase a ball, try one of those rubber balls that are hollow. You can put some food item inside it and the dog will spend time trying to pick the treat out.

Devise other active games to play with your dog. You might even practice obedience activities such as sit, down, and stay. With food rewards, any dog will think training is fun.

Allow your dog time outside the house. If you can provide a fenced area or an area bounded by an electric fence, your dog can be given free time to exercise unrestrained out of doors. If your confinement arrangement is a long chain, your dog can still move about freely. Your dog can have outdoor freedom for hours in good weather, but only if it behaves itself. If your dog is too destructive to leave alone outside, you'll have to allow it out only to eliminate.

A common activity for a dog confined out of doors is— nothing. Many dogs will just curl up on the porch and go to sleep. A dog sleeping outside is not getting any more exercise than a dog sleeping next to your bed.

Take your dog for a ride in the car. Most dogs love to ride. A trip in a car is just amusement, not exercise, but your dog will enjoy it. Never allow your dog to stick its head out of a moving car window. Particles blowing in the wind will damage its eyes.

Get someone else to walk your dog. Maybe there is a local

dog walker you can hire to take Rover for regular outings. The neighbor's kids might like to earn a few dollars working after school as a dog walker. If you do hire a youngster, be sure that he or she can control your dog. If your dog might pull away or grab another child or another dog, better walk it yourself.

Take your dog to a dog park or to doggie day care. If there is a local park where dogs are permitted to run loose and play with other dogs, this might be a good way to allow Rover some freedom and exercise without yourself having to put in many miles. Dog parks are not without some hazards, however. Even though aggressive dogs are not permitted, there is the chance that Rover might tangle with another dog with unfortunate results. Also, many owners at dog parks are not diligent about cleaning up after their dogs; contact with the excrement of other dogs may expose yours to internal parasites. If you do use a dog park or any area frequented by many dogs, have your veterinarian examine your dog's stool for parasite eggs at least twice a year.

Doggie day care establishments have sprung up in some larger metropolitan areas. Professional dog sitters provide care, meals, and amusement for Rover while you are away. Doggie day care is not inexpensive. Unless you have a full-time job that keeps you away from home for long hours, this service is more appropriate for people who would rather spend a good deal of money having others look after their dog than to care for it themselves.

What if I'm handicapped and not able to walk with my dog?

Seniors with walkers, canes, and wheelchairs can be great dog owners! Just because dogs like exercise it doesn't mean that they will be seriously deprived if they don't get much. Consider the guide dog leading a sight-impaired person. The dog and the person are always together, so the dog gets exactly the same amount of activity as its master.

Remember that a dog with limited exercise, just as a human who is relatively inactive, needs fewer calories to stay healthy. Obesity, especially in some of the large breeds, is a serious threat to the health and longevity of dogs.

Provide your relatively inactive dog with lots of toys, and pick up everything that you don't want chewed—a relatively sedentary dog is more likely to find itself some amusement, and I'm sure you'd rather it isn't your shoes.

You can give your dog quite a bit of exercise inside your house. If the dog has any inclination to fetch a ball, provide yourself with two tennis balls. Throw one, and when Rover brings it back and drops it at your feet (or chair), throw the other one. Pick up the first ball while Rover is going for the second. That way, you don't have to grab the ball away from your dog. If you can play fetch up and down stairs, the dog will get a lot of exercise in only a few minutes.

There are professional dog-walking services in many urban areas, but if you live in the suburbs, you might consider hiring a high school student to take your dog a couple of times a week. If there is a dog park nearby, the student could take the dog there for an active playtime. I'll bet the same student who cleans up your yard would like that job, too.

Letting your dog run loose is not an appropriate exercise.

If there is one lesson to be learned, it's that no dog should ever run loose unsupervised or unattended by its owner.

Whenever you see a loose dog, you can consider it to be a dog without a caring owner. Loose dogs get lost, stolen, hit by cars, poisoned, and attacked by other animals. "But my dog never leaves the yard." Don't trust it. It only takes once for your dog to be hit by a car or picked up by a stranger who would like to own a dog like yours.

Of course, there are the rare instances in which a dog escapes confinement in spite of the best efforts of its owner. A dog may run through an electric barrier. It may climb, dig under, or jump a fence. It may break a chain. These situations demonstrate why a dog should always wear an identification tag on its collar. The tag might be its best ticket home.

No dog should get a second chance to escape a confinement area. Once it has climbed a fence, it cannot be trusted not to do it again. If your dog is an escape artist, make other arrangements to keep it safely controlled.

Yes, electric barrier fences are expensive to buy and have installed. Yes, chain-link fences are also expensive, and may be prohibited in some areas. However, dog chains of appropriate length and weight are available at every pet, hardware, and most grocery stores for a few dollars. If you love your dog, don't let it loose.

Chapter 7
Proper Veterinary Care

You have good reason to worry about the veterinary care that your dog needs now and the medical care that it may need in the future. Veterinary medicine today approaches the complexity and expertise of human medicine. Your pet can have its problems diagnosed with multiple laboratory tests, radiographs, surgical biopsies, MRIs, CAT scans, and almost every technique available in a human hospital. Your dog can undergo medical or surgical treatment for a vast array of conditions. Your dog can receive blood transfusions and the latest drugs. Long gone are the days when veterinary treatment meant only "a shot" or "a pill." The result of this huge improvement in veterinary diagnosis and treatment is pets that live longer, healthier, happier lives.

Unfortunately, this great increase in care available to dogs has a negative side: these diagnoses, medications, and procedures usually require the services of specialists and can be very costly. Government programs such as Medicare, Medicaid, and private medical insurance take care of most of the cost for humans. Although pet insurance is available, you are likely to find yourself in the position of having to choose the medical care that your dog will receive on the basis of what you can afford to spend.

The expense of modern medical treatment often is not the only problem. To receive some of these advanced treatments, your dog will have to be transported to and from the medical facility many times, will have to have special care at home, and will probably be given medication for you to administer at home. Transporting and caring for your sick dog can be a major difficulty for some seniors.

Eventually, your dog may need some of these advanced medical procedures to maintain its health or its very life. But there are ways to prevent some (certainly not all) of the most common and devastating problems that can affect your pet and your wallet.

Prevention! Prevention! Prevention!

Keep your dog as healthy as you possibly can. Prevention is much less costly and troublesome and less heartbreaking than is treatment. Save yourself worry, time and money. Follow these five rules:

> Rule Number One: Never allow your dog to run loose where it can get injured, poisoned, lost, or stolen. Keep your dog indoors, on a leash, behind a fence, or on a chain. "HBC" (hit by a car) is the most common notation on a dog trauma patient's record. Avoid the expense of having broken legs repaired, wounds sutured, or poisoning treated. Avoid the heartbreak of searching for and possibly never finding your pet. The cost of preventing your dog from running loose can be as much as a fenced yard or as little as a pet-store chain. The cost of allowing your dog loose can be incalculable both in money and in heartbreak.

What if your dog is determined to sneak out whenever the door is opened? A really clever dog can figure out how to get past you, run into the street, or get lost. There are a few preventive measures you can try to avoid this:

Try using an aversive stimulus, such as your can of compressed air, to teach your dog to stay away from the opened door. Right before you open the door, squirt a little air in the dog's direction and command: Back! Hopefully the dog will learn not to approach the door every time you go to open it.

If you have the patience, put your dog in another room, or in it's Safe Place before you open the door. You'll have to remember to do it every time. If you forget just once, your smart and determined dog might escape.

You could keep your dog from trying to get out the door with the use of an electronic device called a zone barrier. This item is similar to an electronic bark-prevention collar, except that the dog gets a tiny shock when it approaches a forbidden area. The dog wears a receiver collar; a transmitter is placed in the area you want it to avoid. You can buy extra transmitters so that the dog can be kept out of several areas (such as the trash can) with the same receiver collar. Of course, if you use an electronic zone barrier at the door, you'll have to take your dog outside by another door; it will not be willing to approach the forbidden door even id its receiver collar is removed.

> Rule Number Two: Have your dog spayed or neutered while it is young and healthy. Surgery on healthy dogs is not inexpensive, but surgery on sick old dogs is much more costly because of the special care that sick old dogs must receive. In addition to the expense, sick old dogs are at much greater risk of not surviving surgery than are young, healthy dogs.

If your older dog is not spayed or neutered, have it done before it develops some of the reproductive-tract problems of older dogs. If necessary, there are programs that can help you by defraying all or part of the cost. (More information in the Appendix)

> Rule Number Three: Have your dog vaccinated against common infectious diseases. Yes, having your dog vaccinated is another expense. But the treatment for the diseases that can be prevented by vaccination is far more expensive and far less successful than preventing the diseases from the start.

> Rule Number Four: Keep your dog at a normal weight. This is especially true of the large breeds. Orthopedic problems are very common in such dogs as Labrador retrievers and German shepherds. Many, but not all, of these conditions can be prevented or minimized by keeping your dog from becoming overweight. Chapter 8 contains more information about this problem.

> Rule Number Five: Prevent parasite problems. Heartworm and fleas are the major parasitic conditions that affect dogs. Modern medicines prevent both conditions from damaging your dog.

Your dog must be neutered or spayed.

Terms indicating the sexual status of a dog include:

> Altered: has had the reproductive organs surgically removed. Applies to dogs of either sex, occasionally used only for males.
> Castrated: has had the testicles surgically removed.
> Intact: not spayed or neutered; able to reproduce.
> Neutered: same as castrated, altered, or sterilized.
> Spayed: has had the uterus and ovaries surgically removed. The medical term for spayed is an ovariohysterectomy.

Sterilized is the same as altered.

The ability to reproduce is harmful to individual dogs. Overpopulation is harmful to the entire canine species, since millions of homeless dogs are euthanized in shelters every year. Dogs' reproduction is expensive and troublesome for the dog's owner. If the owner is a senior citizen, his dog's reproductive capacities are especially troublesome. Here's why:

Females.

Do you understand the female dog's reproductive cycle? Female dogs that are not spayed have heat periods (estrus) on an average of every six months, starting when they are five to ten months old. Each period last about three weeks. During her heat period, the dog has a messy discharge that stains rugs and furniture. In the last 10 days of her heat period, the dog will attract males to your yard and on the street. If she is not protected from the advances of roaming male dogs, she will be mated and get pregnant.

Your pregnant female will deliver her puppies at the end of an approximately 63-day gestation. Presuming that she has a normal pregnancy and delivery, the puppies will be a messy, expensive nuisance to take care of for about 7 or 8 weeks. Then you will have the duty of providing veterinary care and finding homes for them all.

With care, you can prevent your female dog from being mated and getting pregnant. Keep her away from the male dogs and don't tie her out in the yard and go away; the neighborhood males will find her. But even though your dog doesn't get pregnant, your problems won't be over.

A female dog's normal ovarian hormones are designed to promote maternal behavior after her puppies are born. Even if she is not pregnant, at the end of the normal gestation period of 63 days, your female dog's hormones will cause her to act as though she had given birth to puppies. This condition is called a false pregnancy (pseudocyesis) and can last several weeks. Your dog might hide in dark places, scratch a "nest" in her bed or yours, and even put a toy in her "nest" and growl if you come near it. Most dogs in false pregnancy have some mammary gland development and actually produce milk for their phantom pups.

At least 25 percent of all not-spayed female dogs will develop uterine infections and/or mammary tumors by the time they are 8 to 12 years old. Heat periods and false (or real) puppies are troublesome, but the important reason to have your female dog spayed is for her own health. A female dog's reproductive organs can cause her to have huge, life-threatening problems. A uterine infection (septic metritis) is the most serious. This infection usually occurs about two months after a normal heat period. The infection is very common in older un-spayed dogs that have had multiple heat periods. Unless she undergoes emergency spay surgery and intensive veterinary treatment, septic metritis is likely to be fatal to your dog.

Sick older dogs are very poor surgical risks and may not recover. Surgery on old, sick dogs is much more complicated and expensive than surgery on young, healthy animals. Have your dog spayed while she is a good surgical risk.

Mammary tumors (breast cancer) is the other life-threatening problem facing non-spayed dogs. Just as with humans, dogs with breast cancer need surgery and other treatments to prolong their lives. Just as with uterine infections, it is the older non-spayed dogs that develop this cancer.

Here's the good news: A spayed dog doesn't have heat periods and messy discharges. A spayed dog never has a false pregnancy. A spayed dog has no uterus or ovaries (they were removed when she was spayed) so she never has metritis or ovarian cancer. A dog that was spayed before her first heat period never gets breast cancer. However, after a female dog has had two or three heat periods, spaying will not protect her from mammary tumors. Have your dog spayed when she is as young as possible.

The American Veterinary Medical Association, the largest and most influential group of veterinarians in the country, recommends spaying and neutering dogs as young as six or eight weeks. Extensive research has shown that prepubertal (before puberty: five or six months of age in most dogs) spaying and neutering is the safest for the puppy and the most cost-effective for the owner. Forget what Grandma told you about waiting until a dog has had a heat period or even a litter before having her spayed. Avoid all the trouble and threats to her health; have your dog spayed as soon as you can

Males.

Male dogs don't have "heat" periods as do females. Most male dogs are ready to mate with a receptive female at any time. There are things—even life-endangering things—that can go wrong with a male dog's reproductive system, but these conditions are not as common or often not as serious as those that endanger the lives of affected females. The main reason male house dogs are neutered (castrated, altered) is to prevent some of the unacceptable behaviors of non-neutered males.

Perhaps the mental health of the dog's owner, especially if the owner is a reasonably fussy housekeeper—is the main reason male house dogs should be neutered. Wild dogs such as wolves and coyotes delineate their hunting territories with many, many squirts of their urine throughout the area in which they hunt. This is called "scent marking." Other members of their species are warned away by the scent of the animal that claims the territory as his own.

Domestic dogs inherit the same marking behavior. This is fine when wild dogs mark trees and bushes. It isn't so fine when pet dogs mark drapes and sofas. Marking behavior is entirely governed by sex hormones that are manifest at about six months of age, the start of puberty in male dogs. Even though a few non-spayed female dogs will urine-mark, the behavior is very much more prevalent in non-neutered males. Since the instinct to mark is so strong, punishment is not much of a deterrent to the habitual urine-marker.

The dog that is neutered (or spayed) before puberty doesn't develop the hormones that cause marking behavior. Once a dog has reached puberty and learned the marking habit, few dogs stop urine marking immediately after they are neutered. It may take weeks for the habitual marking behavior to gradually diminish and eventually stop. To avoid this problem altogether, have your dog neutered before puberty. If your dog is already past puberty, it is still worthwhile to have him neutered. Eventually his marking habits will become weak and perhaps stop. If you are the owner of one of the few intact male dogs that have never marked, consider yourself lucky. Have him neutered before his hormones change his behavior for the worst.

In addition to scent marking, there are other behavioral issues that are influenced by neutering. Staying home is not one of them. Don't think that because your dog is neutered, he will sit on the porch all day. Dogs are intelligent, curious creatures; they roam and wander (and get hit by cars) because of their brains, not their reproductive organs. Read Rule Number One: Never let your dog run loose.

Neutering your dog will help diminish his aggressive tendencies toward other dogs. Just as with scent marking, fighting with other dogs is a hormone-influenced learned behavior. Neutering a dog when it is young has the best chance to minimize his fighting tendencies, but even neutering an adult dog is beneficial in this regard.

"But he won't be a watchdog if he's neutered." Wrong. All dogs, male and female, altered or not, inherit the watchdog behavior to some degree. The guard dog instinct is stronger in breeds that have been selected for this trait, such as shepherds and Dobermans, but even a Chihuahua will bark wildly when someone rings the doorbell. Dogs guard their homes and families because of this instinct, not because of their hormones.

Some serious medical conditions threaten the health of male dogs that are not neutered. These conditions are not as common as are the problems of non-spayed female dogs. Tumors of the testicles occur in dogs, especially in dogs that have testicles that have not descended into the normal position in the dog's scrotum. Enlarged prostate glands and cancer of the prostate occur occasionally in not-castrated dogs. Tumors are not uncommon around the anus of a not-neutered dog. These are called perianal adenomas. The growths bleed, become infected, and can be quite messy and debilitating. Some breeds, notably German Shepherds, have a greater tendency than other breeds to be affected by these tumors.

None of these conditions occurs in dogs that are neutered. In fact, perianal adenomas and enlarged prostates regress and often disappear if the affected dog is castrated. Save yourself a lot of trouble and money. Have your dog neutered at as young an age as possible.

Your dog must be vaccinated.

Several potentially fatal canine diseases are common in the dog population. Some of these diseases are world-wide, some are prevalent only in local areas. Viruses and bacteria are the cause of these diseases. Most of these harmful organisms affect only dogs, but some can harm other animals including humans.

Disease-causing organisms can be anywhere. Your healthy dog can contact these organisms in many ways. A sick dog and a healthy dog just touching noses is more than enough to infect the healthy dog. A healthy dog breathing the virus-laden air where a sick dog has been, a healthy dog sniffing the feces or urine of a sick dog, a healthy dog being petted by a person who has petted a sick dog—if any of this happens, your healthy dog is exposed to a potentially fatal condition.

There is no way to isolate your dog from all these exposures. Many sick dogs don't look sick; they are just coming down with the disease or are recovering from it but are still contagious. Modern vaccination methods are the answer. Effective vaccines, correctly administered, will protect more than 90 percent of healthy dogs from catching these deadly diseases.

Vaccines can be divided into two groups: core vaccines and non-core vaccines. Core vaccines are essential for the health of every dog. These are the vaccines that protect dogs against distemper, adenovirus (hepatitis), parvovirus, parainfluenza, leptospirosis, and bordetella, (kennel cough). Often three or more core vaccines are combined in one product. Your dog can be protected against several diseases with one "shot."

Non-core vaccines protect against diseases that are either not common in your area or that your dog is not likely to con-tact. For example, since Lyme disease is spread to dogs by the bite of the deer tick, the administration of a vaccination against

Lyme disease is probably not necessary if you live in a high-rise apartment in New York City. If you live in a wooded area in Pennsylvania, Lyme disease vaccine is advisable.

Your veterinarian must decide which vaccines to give your dog and when your dog needs these vaccines. He or she is in the best position to know what your individual dog should receive.

Always have your dog vaccinated against rabies. Although there is only a slight chance that your dog (it doesn't run loose) will be exposed to a rabid animal, there are reasons that every dog should be vaccinated against rabies.

> Some cities, states, or counties require that every dog be vaccinated against rabies before a license can be purchased for it.

> Injuries caused by dogs must be reported to the local health department. If your dog is vaccinated against rabies and is ever accused of biting or scratching someone, you probably will avoid much of the problems of having your dog quarantined. Keep your rabies vaccination certificate where you can find it.

> Rabies vaccines are very safe, very effective, very long lasting, (three years or more) and relatively inexpensive.

MARTHA

Martha Schmidt was a senior citizen. When her old dog died, she elected to replace it with a young dog from the local humane society. We treated her new dog for roundworms and advised another fecal examination to be sure that the dog was free of the parasites.

When I saw Mrs. Schmidt and her dog in the waiting room, I went out and greeted them. I asked her

to give the fecal sample to the technician to prepare it for examination.

To my surprise, Mrs. Schmidt started to laugh. She couldn't stop laughing. Puzzled, I asked her what was so funny about a stool sample.

Finally, her laughter was reduced to giggles. She choked out, "On my way here, I had to stop at the hardware store to get a wrench set that my husband had ordered. I put my purse on the counter and took out my wallet to pay for the tools." Mrs. Schmidt started to chuckle again. "Somebody stole my purse!"

"What's so funny about having your purse stolen?" I asked.

She was laughing so hard that it was hard to understand her. Finally I figured out what she was trying to say "I had my wallet in my hand. The only other thing in that old purse was—the stool sample."

How do I prevent parasite problems?

Parasites are organisms that live on the skin or inside the body of another animal. Parasites can cause considerable problems. Modern medications make it possible to prevent or eliminate nearly all parasites from your dog.

Heartworm is the most serious parasitic disease that affects dogs. As the name indicates, heartworms are actual worms that live in the heart and major blood vessels of affected dogs. Heartworms are spread from affected dogs to unaffected ones by mosquitoes. When a mosquito sucks up some blood from a dog with heartworm, it gets some of the larvae of the heartworm that are circulating in the sick dog's blood. When the same mosquito bites an unaffected dog, the mosquito injects some of the heartworm larvae into that dog.

The larvae of the heartworm, called microfilaria, migrate in the body of the newly infected dog, eventually maturing as worms in the dog's heart and vessels. Mature worms produce more microfilaria that circulate through the dog's bloodstream and are ingested by mosquitoes that bite the dog. Mature heartworms can grow to several inches long; they cause damage by obstructing the normal flow of blood. Eventually, the affected dog can die of circulatory failure.

In spite of the severity of heartworm disease, modern medications make it relatively easy to prevent, and even to treat in the early stages. Your veterinarian will test your dog's blood to see if it is free of heartworm. If your dog is negative for heartworm, your veterinarian will prescribe tablets to be given to your dog once a month. These tablets prevent the heartworm microfilaria from living in your dog's blood.

If an examination of your dog's blood indicates that it has a heartworm infection, it can be treated for the condition. If the dog is not clinically sick, it is almost certain that it will recover with treatment. Even dogs that are moderately sick from heartworm usually can be treated successfully. When infected dog is free of heartworm, it is given the monthly preventive medication to keep it from getting the condition again.

Intestinal parasites: (worms).

Roundworms are present in the intestines of nearly every puppy. Puppies get the parasite from their mothers before they are born. Puppies may even pass adult roundworms, which are easy to see—they look like spaghetti. All puppies should be treated several times to eliminate this parasite.

Adult dogs can get roundworms by accidentally eating infective ova (eggs) of the parasite. Soil contaminated with fecal material of infected dogs is the common source of roundworm infection in older dogs.

The immature stages of roundworms can affect humans, especially children who are not careful about what goes into their mouths. Be careful. If you have a puppy or young dog and grandchildren who love to play with it, have the children wash their hands very well when they are finished playing.

Tapeworms actually look like a tape: long and flat. These parasites are made of short segments. The end segments break off and often appear on an infected dog's stool or stuck to the hair around its anus. You can see these segments: when they are first passed, the segments move; later they look like dried-up grains of rice.

The tapeworm must live in two different animals, called hosts, to complete its life cycle. In the case of the common tapeworm of dogs and cats, this other host is the flea. Fleas cause dogs to itch, and to chew and lick themselves. When your dog licks up and accidentally swallows an infected flea, it becomes infected with tapeworms. Obviously, the way to keep your dog free of tapeworms is to keep it free of fleas.

Yes, humans can get tapeworms, but not dog tapeworms. You and your grandchildren are in no danger of getting tapeworms from your dog.

Hookworms, whipworms, and coccidia are other parasites that can infect your dog. These organisms are too small to be seen with the naked eye. They can only be seen under a microscope, so your veterinarian must detect these infections by examining your dog's stool.

The most common sign of intestinal parasite infection other than tapeworm in a dog is diarrhea. If your adult dog has diarrhea occasionally, it is probably from something it ate, not parasites. Your veterinarian will include a microscopic check of its stool in the dog's routine examination, but if your dog has diarrhea very often, have its stool checked again.

"Worm medicine" is poison. It kills worms. Never dose your dog with pet store products just because it has diarrhea. Never dose your dog "just in case it has worms." The use of the wrong vermifuge ("worm medicine") or the wrong dose can be dangerous to your dog.

Many over-the-counter products that you can buy in pet stores and in the pet isles of grocery stores are old drugs that have been used for years to treat internal parasites in dogs. New drugs, many only available only from your veterinarian, eliminate internal parasites much more effectively and with much less harm to your dog than do those old products. Your veterinarian will prescribe the correct new drug at the correct dose only after determining if your dog has internal parasites and what kind of parasites it has.

A warning: tapeworms are the only internal parasite that you may be able to diagnose yourself when you find the tapeworm segments on your dog. Don't treat your dog with over-the-counter tapeworm medicine. Old-formula OTC tapeworm medicine causes extreme diarrhea and vomiting; that's how it gets the tapeworms out of the dog. Your veterinarian's prescription tapeworm medicine will eliminate this parasite from your dog without any bad effects at all. Over-the-counter "worm medicine" for dogs can be dangerous and ineffective. OTC medication for tapeworms is especially hazardous. Get the right medication from your veterinarian.

Skin parasites.

Fleas are the most common and the most troublesome skin

parasites of dogs. You'll probably know if your dog has fleas: it frequently scratches and licks itself. You can examine your dog and see fleas running through the hair and sometimes jumping off the dog.

The life cycle of the flea includes flea eggs and flea larvae on the ground—usually in the carpet, the dog's bed, or where it likes best to sleep. Since fleas are a constant source of irritation to your dog and the source of tapeworms, it is important to eliminate this parasite.

Even if you can't see fleas on your dog, if it scratches more than just occasionally, fleas are probably there. Be safe: use flea-control products if you even suspect that your dog might be infested.

Your dog doesn't have to have fleas. In the past, it was very difficult to get rid of all the fleas on pets. Old methods of flea control involved flea soap, flea powder, flea combs, and flea spray for the dog, as well as chemicals to treat the dog's environment. In recent years, flea control has taken a giant step forward.

You no longer have to cover your dog with flea powder or scrub it with special soap. Modern medications are easy to use and, if used correctly, will eliminate all fleas. New flea and tick products are absorbed into the dog's system. These products kill or prevent the reproduction of all fleas and ticks that bite the dog.

There are two types of modern flea and tick medications: one is given by mouth in the form of tablets. The other is applied to the dog's skin in a single spot on the back of the dog's neck. To be effective, these products must be used at regular intervals, usually once a month.

Your veterinarian can supply the best and most effective flea killing products. Some of these products also include medication to prevent other parasites such as heartworms. You can buy flea-controlling medications of many types over-the-counter at pet stores. Some of these OTC products, especially the brands that are applied to the dog's skin, will be effective if the directions are followed very carefully. Since the over-the-counter flea products from a pet shop and the prescription flea killers from your veterinarian are quite similar in cost, it might be advisable to get your veterinarian's product and advice.

Other types of skin parasites.

Ticks can carry diseases that affect humans, such as Rocky Mountain Spotted Fever and Lyme disease. Dog ticks are blood-sucking creatures. Male and unfed female ticks are very small, but blood-filled females of the common dog tick may be as big as the end of your index finger. Female ticks drop off your dog and lay thousands of eggs in the environment. If you suspect that your dog has ticks, examine the insides of its ears and between its toes. These are the areas preferred by the ticks.

Ticks are harder to kill than fleas. Many products will kill both fleas and ticks, but the fleas will be gone long before the ticks die. It may take days after the chemicals are applied before the ticks are killed.

Lice are uncommon on dogs. These tiny white creatures are stationary; they don't move through the dog's hair as do fleas. Lice are easy to kill, but louse eggs adhere to hair shafts and are hard to remove. It is unlikely that you will ever see lice on your dog, but if you do, don't worry about catching them yourself. Lice are very fussy about where they live. Dog lice won't live on people.

All Mange Mites are microscopic in size and can only be identified under a microscope. Mites that affect dogs are of three varieties: sarcoptic, demodectic, and ear mites.

Sarcoptic mites cause intense itching and scratching. These mites may be very hard to find on dogs' skin. If your dog scratches all the time and your veterinarian cannot find another cause, he or she may treat the dog for sarcoptic mange as a precaution. Once diagnosed, sarcoptic mange is not difficult to cure.

Ear mites often cause a dog to scratch its ears until it damages its ear flaps. Ear mites cause the ear canal to become filled with dark, smelly wax. Your veterinarian can show you the mites under the microscope in a bit of this wax. Ear mites are often transmitted to dogs by infected cats or other dogs. Old medications and OTC products can be used to treat ear mites, but modern medications from your veterinarian make ear mite elimination easy, often with a single treatment.

Demodectic mange mites are transmitted only from a mother dog to her puppies. A mother dog may have no signs of the disease but still may have demodectic mites in her skin that infect her nursing puppies. Older dogs and puppies more than four weeks of age are very resistant to catching these mites. A recently appearing skin condition in your adult dog is very unlikely to be domodic mange.

Suspect demodex (demodectic mange) if your very young dog has bald spots around its lips or on its front feet. Surprisingly, demodex does not cause the patient to scratch very much.

Demodectic mange often is self-limiting and will go away in time. Other cases can become very severe and result in the dog's entire body becoming involved. Before the availability of modern drugs, dogs badly affected with demodex often were euthanized. Today, new medications can treat all cases of demodex, although it may take quite a bit of treatment to control the condition. Demodectic mange always needs to be treated by your veterinarian.

Ringworm is more common on cats than on dogs, and can be transmitted to humans. Children are especially subject to catching ringworm from pets. If unusual bald spots appear on your dog, show them to your veterinarian. It may take an examination under a special light and a skin culture to confirm or eliminate the presence of ringworm.

How to apply flea and tick products to your dog's skin.

Topical medications to kill fleas and ticks are supplied in little capsules. The size of the dog that can be treated by each capsule is indicated on the package.

Each capsule has a little spout. Snip the spout with a scissors to release the medication. Part the hair on the back of the dog's neck to expose the skin. Squeeze the entire contents of the capsule onto the dog's skin. Try to avoid wasting some of the chemical by getting it on the hair; it must be on the dog's skin to be absorbed and to be effective.

The medication is applied to the back of dogs' necks because dogs cannot lick themselves in that spot. Instruct your grandchildren not to touch the medicated area on your dog. If your grandchildren are very small, apply the flea and tick killing medication when the children will not be in contact with the dog for at least 12 hours, or until the medication is completely absorbed by the dog's skin.

These "one-spot" flea and tick medications are designed to be re-applied at four-week intervals. In some cases, the products will have to be applied more frequently. Your veterinarian will advise you.

How to give your dog tablets or capsules by mouth.

There's no need to struggle to give your dog a "pill." All you need is a soft, tasty treat to wrap the medication. A slice of hotdog or a piece of soft cheese like Velveeta works very well, as does liver sausage or canned cat food. You may have to stick the point of a knife into the treat to make an opening to insert the tablet or capsule. If you are giving a large capsule, it is easiest to use something like hamburger that can be molded around the medication.

First give your dog a piece of the treat without the medication to show it how good it tastes. Then give the dog another piece in which you have inserted the tablet or capsule. Have another un-medicated piece ready. The dog will gulp down the medicated piece to reach for the new piece.

How to give your dog liquid medicine.

Many preparations for dogs, especially for small dogs, are furnished as liquids in dropper bottles. If your dog is co-operative at all and the medication is only a small volume, you can stick the end of the dropper into the side of its mouth and squirt the medication directly onto the dog's tongue.

If the liquid medication has a strong taste or odor, or the dog must be given more than a single dropper-full, it will be more difficult to administer. If you just try to pour the liquid medicine into your dog's mouth, you might accidentally get some of it in the dog's trachea and lungs. Or the dog will shake its head and spatter at least part of its dose onto your best sweater. You'll have to try a little trickery.

Put the medication on a small piece of bread. A dose of

about two cubic centimeters (two to four droppers-full) will require half a slice of ordinary grocery store bread.

After the medication has soaked into the bread, "butter" the bread with something the dog really likes such as cheese spread, goose liver sausage, or cat food. Regular butter or margarine doesn't have enough smell or taste to attract most dogs. Unless your dog eagerly grabs the medicated bread, feed the bread into small pieces.

Chapter 8
Feeding Your Dog

Walk down the dog food isle at the local super market. All those choices. The dog food industry in the United States is a multi-billion dollar business. There are more different items to select from than there are in the human cereal isle. Choosing the right food for your dog takes a lot of thought and consideration.

Pet foods sold in the United States must be labeled according to the regulations of the Association of American Feed Control Officials (AAFCO). AAFCO requires that pet food labels include the guaranteed analysis of minimum crude protein, minimum crude fat, maximum crude fiber, and maximum moisture content of each product. Also required is a statement of nutritional adequacy. When a label claims a food to be "complete and balanced nutrition," the manufacturer is required to substantiate that claim by meeting the AAFCO standards.

Dry Dog Foods.

Modern dry dog foods are sold as pellets of various sizes and shapes, produced by extruding cooked meal through dies.

Dry dog foods are designed to be fed straight from the bag or moistened with liquid. These foods can be purchased in many size packages, from two-pound boxes to 50-pound sacks. Dry foods are supplied as "puppy," "adult maintenance," "adult active," "senior dog," "weight loss," "weight maintenance," and many, many special formulas.

Dry dog foods are divided into popular brands sold in grocery stores, premium formulae of national brands, and economy or generic brands. The protein, fat, fiber, and moisture contents of these foods are calculated on dry basis. The maximum moisture content of this type of food is usually about 12 percent.

Canned dog foods.

Dog food can be purchased in cans as adult diets, puppy diets, "small dog" diets, and all-meat formulae. Large cans of dog food usually contain 15.5 ounces, small ones, five and a half ounces. The small cans of food are sold on the basis of greater palatability where cost is not a factor when feeding a very small dog. All-meat formulae are used to mix with other forms of food to improve the taste. Canned dog foods often contain 80 percent or more water.

Semi-moist forms.

Corn syrup is the main preservative in semi-moist forms of dog food. This type of food is quite tasty to dogs and quite attractive to owners who feel they are giving their dogs something that looks like meat. These foods are convenient to feed; often they are supplied in cellophane single-serving bags and require no refrigeration. Semi-moist foods are usually about 30 percent water.

Dog treats.

Meaty strips, chunks, biscuits, or pellets are usually semi-moist products sold in small quantities in boxes or bags. Since these make up only a small portion of a dog's die, get whatever your dog likes best.

Which type of food should I choose for my dog?

Convenience and economy—these are two factors to consider when you choose a type of food for your dog. If you have a medium or large dog, dry food is the best choice. Buy the largest package that you can handle and store easily, since the price per pound is the least in the larger packages.

If you have a very small dog, convenience might be more important than economy. Little dogs consume such a small amount of food that you might overlook the cost. Canned and semi-moist dog foods are always less economical than the dry forms, since you are paying for the water in the food and the more expensive packages or cans.

It's tempting to feed your dog Tiny all meat-canned dog food, or real meat such as hamburger or chicken, since that's what he loves to eat. Tiny might even refuse to eat anything except chicken or meat. Don't let him get away with that! All-meat diets are not nutritionally adequate for dogs of any size or age.

Should I buy the most expensive brands?

Premium brands are more expensive than popular brands, and often twice as costly as economy brands. The difference between popular, premium, and economy dog foods is the quality of ingredients and the amount of indigestible fiber in the product. Think of premium brands as more concentrated nutrition. Premium brands contain the most digestible material, the greatest number of calories per cupful, and require the dog be fed a smaller quantity of food to get the same nutritional value. Because they contain less indigestible material, the dog that is fed premium brands of food will have smaller and less frequent stools than the one fed a brand that contains more indigestible fiber.

A normal adult pet dog doesn't need to be fed premium food. The better popular brands of dog food meet all of the AAFCO standards and are formulated to be nutritionally adequate for the average dog. Although these foods may contain somewhat more indigestible material, the difference in the amount of feed needed to nourish your dog and the volume of its stool is not very significant. Unless your dog has a problem related to its diet, choose a good national brand.

Economy, generic, or grocery store private brands of dry or canned dog food are a very poor choice. These foods are sold on price alone. They are composed of the cheapest ingredients, contain the most indigestible matter, and do not meet AAFCO standards for providing "complete and balanced nutrition" for your dog. You won't find that statement on the bag.

A dog that is fed economy food will need to eat from 1 ½ to twice as much food just to maintain its weight. The increase in the amount of economy food needed by your dog eliminates the saving in money over buying a better grade of dog food and feeding a smaller amount.

If you feed economy or generic brands of dog food, your dog will have larger, softer, and more frequent bowel movements. One study showed that dogs fed economy grade dog food had three times the volume of fecal matter than dogs fed the premium grades. Not only is this three times the amount of droppings to pick up in your yard, it is three times the number of times your dog must go out to eliminate.

If you are tempted to buy generic or economy canned dog food just because your dog likes the canned stuff more, you better buy only one can. The minute you open it and take a sniff, you'll change your mind. That stuff is made of leftovers from the processing of other foods, and often smells like what it is—not fit for human (or canine) consumption. Standard and premium brands of canned dog food often smell like you'd serve them on crackers to your bridge club. I don't recommend doing this but you know what I mean.

What about special formulas?

Many of the popular brands and some of the premium brands offer "senior" and "light" formulae dog foods as well as "puppy" and "adult maintenance." "Light" is a term meaning reduced in calories; this designation is also applied to human foods such as "light" beer. Applied to dog food, "senior" means the same thing: lower in calories. These foods are reduced in calories only about 25 percent over the standard foods. If your dog is too fat and you can't bring yourself to reduce its amount of food, you can give it a few less calories in if you feed the light or senior formulae.

Chicken, lamb, and rice dog foods are formulated for dogs that have allergies to the most common ingredients of regular dog food: beef, wheat, and corn. These foods are intended to eliminate the most common sign of food allergy in dogs: excessive skin scratching. However, if your dog scratches its skin a lot, it is very much more likely that it is allergic to its fleas than to its food. Only a veterinarian can diagnose a true food allergy with skin tests or elimination diets.

Chicken, lamb, or rice diets that are sold in grocery stores often include some beef, wheat, or corn in the formulae. These diets will not reduce true food allergies in dogs, since the food still contains some of the substances that cause the allergies. If your veterinarian has diagnosed your dog with a food allergy, be sure you read the list of ingredients on the bag of food before you buy it. Since most chicken, lamb, or rice dog foods are made by reputable manufacturers and are complete and balanced diets for dogs, there is nothing wrong with feeding these foods to your dog if it does not have a food allergy. Your dog might like and even digest the chicken, lamb, or rice formulae better than the standard foods.

What are prescription diets?

Prescription diets are special-formula foods that are recommended and sold only by veterinarians. These products are designed to minimize certain health problems of pets. There are prescription diets low in roughage for dogs with some types of diarrhea. There are prescription diets very restricted in calories for obese dogs. There are prescription diets with high-quality, restricted-quantity protein for dog with kidney disease. Prescription diets are available in canned or dry forms. You can't buy prescription diet dog foods at a grocery store or at a pet store, although those outlets may sell commercial foods designed for similar health problems.

Prescription diets are among the most expensive of dog foods. If your veterinarian recommends a prescription diet, ask how long your dog will need to eat the diet, and if the dog is allowed any other food in addition to the diet. It is appropriate to ask if there are any commercial alternative foods that are less expensive to feed. Often a premium or even a popular dog food will do the same job as a prescription food at a greatly reduced cost. For example, you can feed a commercial premium dry puppy food to a growing dog just as successfully but far less expensively than you can feed a canned prescription puppy food.

In some cases, only the correct prescription diet will help the patient. For example, if your dog is diagnosed with bladder stones, your veterinarian may recommend a prescription diet that contains the proper mineral content to dissolve the stones over time. You may be able to avoid surgery for your dog by feeding this prescription diet exclusively for months, but there is no commercial or home-made diet that can be substituted successfully to treat this problem.

Should I give my dog supplements?

No, don't give your dog supplements. It's as simple as that. You don't need to add anything if you feed your dog a good quality food. Vitamins and minerals are not expensive ingredients to add to foods. Manufacturers of reliable brands make certain that their products contain adequate amounts of both, so that their foods can be certified as " complete and balanced nutrition."

"But my grandchild gets those chewable vitamins every day. Why not my dog?" Children's diets vary a great deal more than dogs' diets. Dogs welcome the same food every day, but some children refuse to eat food items that are required for them to have complete and balanced diets, so parents supplement children's diets with commercial vitamin products. You can even disturb the correct vitamin and mineral content of your dog's diet by over supplementation. Buy your dog a nutritious brand of food and save your money on the supplements.

Can my dog eat human food as treats, additives or as a complete diet?

Small amounts of human food are just fine as treats for your dog. Many dogs will eat almost anything if they see their owners enjoying the food. This includes fruit, vegetables, and baked goods as well as meat. The amount of human food added to your dog's regular meal should not be greater than ten percent of the total amount that your dog eats.

If your dog is a good eater, you can add human leftovers to its regular meal, just to make its dinner more interesting If your dog tends to reject its good, wholesome dog food, it is probably not a good idea to flavor the food with human scraps. Your dog is likely to learn to turn up its nose to its regular food when no scraps are available.

Don't try to feed your dog a complete diet of human food, no matter how small a dog you have. Even if you go to a great deal of trouble and expense to try to formulate a nutritious diet for your dog out of human food products, you can't do as good a job as the major dog food manufacturers.

How much should I feed my dog?

There is so much difference between individual dogs and between types and brands of dog food that it isn't possible to make rules about how much your dog should be fed. Its size, its age, and its level of activity determine how many calories your dog uses each day. Your dog's breed might influence its caloric needs also. Some breeds, notably the larger ones, seem to have a lower metabolic rate and need less food per pound of body weight than do smaller breeds. Puppies need more food for normal growth than adult dogs do for maintenance.

Feed your dog just enough to keep it on the thin side of normal. That's how we all want to be—thin—but that's not what we all achieve. Sometimes our appetites get in our way of our better judgment, but our dogs have the advantage in this regard: we humans dispense the food. Your dog can't serve itself a second helping or go to the refrigerator for a snack.

You should be able to feel, but not see your dog's ribs. You should be able to see a "waist" right behind its ribs when you look at your dog from above and from the side. If you have a very long-haired dog, you might have to feel for its "waist."

The recommendation on the label of a product is only a very rough estimate of how much of the food your dog should receive. Most adult pet dogs need be fed the lower volume recommended on the label. Read the label, but don't believe everything you read.

Snacks: calories count.

Don't forget about the extras. "But I only feed him once a day" doesn't count the little bites of toast in the morning, the few dog biscuits when he comes in from his walk, and the leftovers from your bedtime snack. If you give your dog treats, you'll need to reduce the amount you feed at its regular meals.

When and how often should I feed my dog?

We've been conditioned to expect three meals a day, but dogs have no such expectations. Wild canines gorge on food whenever it is available, and may go days without another meal.

It is a tradition to feed dogs either once or twice a day. Either is satisfactory. Some dogs will eat only once a day. A dog will normally eliminate soon after it has eaten, so plan your dog's mealtimes for when it is convenient for your schedule to prepare its food, feed it, and then take it out.

What should I never give my dog to eat or chew?

Your dog's opinion of what is good to eat is often vastly different from your opinion. Most dogs will gobble up things that you wouldn't touch even if you were starving. Dogs have an instinct remaining from the time before they were domesticated that tells them "if it might be food, I'd better eat it, because food is hard to get."

Dogs have a much stronger vomiting reflex than do humans. This reflex undoubtedly saves dogs from a lot of digestive problems. If a dog eats something harmful, it is likely to bring it back up within a short time. That is why one bout of simple vomiting is not a sign of a serious disturbance in a dog; its stomach is rejecting a harmful substance.

"Natural" chew toys.

Many products are sold as chew toys on grocery store shelves. Items such as pig ears, cattle hooves, and rawhide in various forms are relished by dogs but are not digestible. Most of these items are relatively harmless to your dog, but won't be harmless to your carpet when your dog vomits them back up, along with the rest of its stomach contents. Personally, I don't like the idea of purchasing offal to give to my dog.

Plastic, rubber, and cloth toys.

If your dog can chew a toy into pieces and swallow the pieces, the toys are in the same category as pig ears—not a good idea. Vomiting is the least harmful of the many problems. Pieces of plastic, rubber, or cloth can block your dog's intestinal tract and might require surgery to save your dog's life.

Nylon bones are relatively safe because they are made of such tough material that even dogs with strong jaws can chew off only small fragments. However, when your dog has chewed a nylon bone down to a small piece, thrown it away before it can be swallowed. Real beef shin bones sold for dog toys are heat-treated to make them very hard and relatively safe. Throw these away when they are reduced to small pieces.

If you have more than one dog, it might be a poor idea to get them any sort of toys that resemble food. Competition over food items is a major cause of dogs' fighting. Avoid the problem altogether. Get only toys that don't smell like they are food.

Some dogs never destroy their toys; some demolish even the sturdiest items in a matter of minutes. You must be the judge of what are safe toys for your dog.

You will hear that chocolate is deadly to dogs. This is in the category of an old wives' tale. Your dog is not going to drop over dead from eating part of a Hershey bar, or even from stealing a few brownies off the table. However, chocolate contains theobromine, a chemical similar to the caffeine in coffee; the darker the chocolate, the more of the chemical is present. Dark, unsweetened chocolate contains the most theobromine. A small dog that eats a pound of dark unsweetened baking chocolate or an entire box of unsweetened cocoa powder will get quite sick, but neither of these products is very tasty, even to dogs. Even though a little chocolate will do it no more harm than it would do you, there is no reason to give your dog chocolate in any form.

If an item would harm you if you ate it, it will probably

harm your dog. The veterinary profession often deals with a condition in dogs called Thanksgiving stomach (sometimes called Christmas stomach). This is vomiting and diarrhea caused by dogs being fed a "treat" of a large amount of greasy turkey skins the day after the holiday meal. Never give your dog large amounts of human leftovers, spoiled food, or anything you wouldn't eat yourself.

It is not an old wives' tale that bones of any kind are harmful for dogs to eat. Bone fragments can pierce dog's intestines and cause possibly fatal internal damage. Bone fragments can become lodged in intestines and produce blockages that require major veterinary attention. Cover your garbage or keep it where Rover can't reach it!

My dog refuses to eat the food it should. What should I do?

Picky eaters are a problem in over-indulged dogs, usually small ones because it is much less expensive to over-indulge a Chihuahua than a Great Dane. If your dog refuses to eat its correct diet, you or its former owner let it learn that something tastier will be offered.

None of us likes to starve our dogs into eating, but your dog will not be well nourished on a diet that consists only of meat or treats. Try your picky eater on a different form of food such as canned or semi-moist instead of dry. If you find a type or brand that it likes and that contains the nourishment that it needs, feed that exclusively at first. Then add this food to its regular diet, in decreasing amounts, gradually cutting down until your dog is getting mostly the food it had previously refused.

Try the same method for a dog that will eat only meat or chicken. Cut up the meat into small pieces and mix it with some good dog food, probably a semi-moist or canned variety. Within two weeks, the dog should accept the food without added meat or chicken.

How about digestive problems?

Dogs are just like people in so many ways. If we, or our dogs, indulge in the wrong thing or in too much of the right thing, both dogs and humans can have problems with our digestive tracts. These problems are more common in dogs, since most dogs are much less fussy about what they consider to be edible than are most humans.

Does my dog need medical attention for its digestive problems?

Is your dog really sick or does it just have a little indigestion? If your dog vomits once or has a soft stool, it is not likely to be a serious problem. But consider the following:

> If your dog is listless, inactive, reluctance to move, or whines when forced to move, it could have a very bad condition such as a foreign body in its intestines.

> If your dog refuses to eat anything, even its most favorite food, suspect a serious condition.

> If your dog vomits more than two or three times, or retches without bringing up anything except a little fluid, it could have gastritis, a serious disturbance in its stomach.

> If your dog has a bloated abdomen, especially if it is reluctant to move or even to lie down, it could have a twisted intestinal tract. This is an emergency. Gas retained in the dog's stomach will cause the dog to die of shock within hours unless

treated very promptly.

> If your dog has a fever of above 103, it is showing signs of infection. You can take your dog's temperature with a human rectal thermometer, just as you would take the temperature of a baby. You can't tell if a dog has a fever by feeling its nose.

> If your dog has uncontrolled watery diarrhea, especially if its stool contains blood or dark, foul-smelling material that could be blood, your dog needs immediate veterinary attention.

> If your dog strains many times but cannot move its bowels, it could have a large intestine impacted with material that cannot be passed. Straining is especially serious if only a little liquid (or even blood) comes out.

> If your dog has signs of disturbance in its nervous system, such as shaking, trembling, convulsions, or collapse, rush it to medical help and hope you will be in time. Nervous system disturbances are often the signs of poisoning.

If you even suspect that your dog has any of these problems, get it to your veterinarian at once.

How can I tell when my dog's digestive problems are not serious?

If your dog has only minor digestive problems, it will be just as active as if it had no problems at all. It will want to eat its usual meal, or at least will accept treats readily. If it vomits, it will vomit only once or twice and act normal thereafter.

If diarrhea is your dog's problem, it is minor if its stool is unformed but neither watery nor especially foul-smelling. Your dog with a minor bout of diarrhea will need to eliminate frequently but will have some control of its bowels.

The dog that appears to have a single difficult bowel movement may have simple constipation. If it strains for more than a few times, it is something worse. If you have a long-haired dog, check to be sure that it doesn't have a mass of fecal material stuck in the hair around its anus. A mass of hardened feces can block it anus and prevent a dog from moving its bowels at all. Many people don't notice this, despite the accompanying odor.

What should I do for my dog with minor digestive problems?

If your dog is frisky and wants its treats in spite of a single episode of vomiting, you might not have to do much. Don't feed your dog for about four hours after it vomits, to be sure that the material that caused the vomiting is completely out of its stomach. Give it only half of its usual amount of food at its next meal and watch it closely to be sure that the vomiting does not continue.

For simple diarrhea, withhold your dog's next meal and let its intestines have a rest. Reduce its usual amount of food for subsequent meals until its stool is normal again. If your dog acts normal but has a chronic soft stool, better check with your veterinarian. The dog may have intestinal parasites, you may be feeding it too much, or you may be feeding it something that its intestines can't handle.

A dog with simple constipation will strain to move its bowels, but will actually pass some fecal material. A dig with a more serious bowel blockage will strain many times, may pass a little fluid or even blood, and will act as though it is in pain. If you even suspect a serious problem, call your veterinarian.

Never give the constipated dog a human laxative product. Many of these products are deadly to dogs.

Part III: Handling Problems

Chapter 9
When You Have a Handicap

How can I care for my dog if I use a walker? If I have poor vision? If I am hard of hearing? Seniors who have limited mobility or limited visual acuity still want and need their dogs. Handicapped seniors have even greater need for their canine companions when many other factors of their lives become limited. How can seniors keep their dogs without compromising their safety and convenience?

How can I keep my dog from causing me to fall?

The biggest fear, both of seniors and of their families, is that the dog will cause the senior to stumble, fall and be hurt. This is not an idle fear; a fall that a younger person would shake off can cause serious damage to a senior. A major fracture such as a broken hip or thigh-bone, or even an arm bone or wrist fracture, can be a permanently disabling event in a senior's life.

Few people value the companionship of their dogs more than seniors with limited mobility. Rover is there to talk to even when the grandchildren are too busy. Rover is company when there's nothing worth watching on TV. But Rover must not be allowed to be the cause of a dangerous fall.

What if I use a cane, crutches or walker?

Of course, we all want our dogs to love us, not to fear us. However, you cannot live in dread that Rover will be underfoot and cause you to stumble or fall whenever you move around. Nobody can remember all of the time to be cautious because Rover might be in the way. One accident might be one too many.

If you use a cane, crutches, or a walker, your dog must be taught to avoid the device and must be taught to avoid you when you are using the device. This is easy to do. Dogs have an instinct to keep away from objects that look threatening. Make the object a real threat to your dog at the proper time.

Whether you use a cane, a walker, or crutches, the procedure for training your dog to avoid your mobility-assistance device is the same. No, never hit your dog with your cane or anything else. Don't even shove your dog away with a cane or a walker; some dogs will consider this an attack or an invitation to play and will grab the cane or walker out of your hands. Teach your dog to avoid the cane or walker only when you are standing or walking with it. When you are seated, the dog will regard the cane as harmless; when you are standing, the cane is dangerous.

How can I train my dog to stay away from my cane, crutches or walker?

Use an avoidance device. Teaching your dog to stay away when you are using your walker or cane is almost identical to teaching your dog not to jump up on you. Use a device such as a pressurized can of air, just as you did when you taught Rover not to jump on you. Keep the can near you for several days;

you want to teach your dog that it always must get out of the way when you are moving with the walker.

Your dog must learn to be cautious about the walker or cane, not to be afraid of you. Stand up holding the walker or cane. Don't say a word. When the dog approaches, say nothing, but squirt it with the canned air. At first, use several quick squirts. If possible, pound the walker on the floor, making as much noise as possible. Take a couple of steps; if the dog hasn't retreated several feet, squirt it again. This sounds unkind, but it is effective. For your safety, you must teach your dog to stay out of the way of your walker or cane.

Go to another chair and sit down. Set the walker or cane aside and call the dog to you, maybe with a little treat. Wait a few minutes. Place the walker in position in front of you, stand up, and squirt the canned air in the direction of the dog even if it isn't very near. A few repetitions and the dog will jump away whenever you get up with your walker. This is exactly what you want; your dog must never cause you to fall by getting underfoot of you and your walker.

Never offer your dog a treat, not even a kind word, when you are standing using your walker. It must learn to stay away. Save the goodies and the praise for the times that you are seated and the walker is set aside.

Reinforce the dog's habit of avoiding your walker or cane every day for the next two weeks. A squirt of air in the direction of the dog is all that you'll need. Soon there will be no way your dog will voluntarily approach you when you are standing or walking with your walker. Even if your dog is asleep in the hallway, he'll wake and dash away when he hears the walker tapping along the floor. You won't fall over your dog because it won't ever be in your path.

Unfortunately, it is not a good idea to take your dog for a

walk outdoors if you must use a cane or a walker. The exceptions include a very tiny dog or one that is especially trained never to pull on the leash. The last thing you want is for your dog to drag you down or to jerk the leash away from your hands.

What if I use a wheelchair?

When you're seated in a wheelchair, your dog can't do you much harm. You can't trip over your dog when you're in a wheelchair. The only problem you'll have is that your dog might try to jump into your lap or to put its feet up on you. If you don't want your dog jumping on you, use that squirt of air again; Rover will soon learn not to jump

You need not teach Rover to be afraid of your wheelchair. Rover will learn to keep himself out of the way when you are moving without any training on your part at all.

You can "walk" your dog outdoors using your wheelchair, if your dog is wearing the correct collar. Assistance dogs have been trained to pull wheelchairs, mainly for children. A big dog can pull even an adult. When it pulls a chair, the dog wears a harness with a leash for pulling as well as a leash attached to its regular collar. The occupant of the wheelchair holds the pulling leash in his hands; he never ties it to the wheelchair.

If you use a motorized wheelchair or a motorized scooter, you have one of the best devices to exercise your dog. You can ride in comfort while Rover walks or runs along side. If Rover is afraid of the chair in motion, start moving very slowly while coaxing him to come along. Use food treats to encourage him. Most dogs will soon decide that going for a "walk" with a chair is a lot of fun.

My vision is impaired.

If you're sightless or partly sightless, it certainly is possible to trip over Rover when you're just walking in your own house. This is the toughest situation for a handicapped person to solve. Even many people with normal vision (myself included) have had a few tumbles over a big black Labrador sound asleep in a dark doorway.

The problem of not being able to see your dog is most important in your own house. When you know the feeling of every room and every wall, you navigate largely by touching familiar landmarks. You won't notice if Rover is in the way. For safety, make it a habit to use your cane when you walk in places where your dog is likely to be lying. You can feel the floor in front of you and detect Rover before you fall over him.

If you have partial vision, you'll be more successful with a white or light-colored dog. This is something to keep in mind if you're getting a new dog, but not helpful if your present Rover is a dark color. Consider getting a white harness or white blanket to make your black dog more conspicuous. Get in the habit of turning on all the lights before you enter a room.

It might be helpful to have a bell on the collar so that the sound will help you locate your dog. Use a bell like a small cowbell, made for hunting dogs' collars. Those little bells on cat collars don't make enough noise.

I am hearing impaired.

Limited hearing, or even complete deafness, is not a handicap to dog ownership. In fact, a noisy watchdog may be a great safety device if you are not able to hear strangers approach your house or apartment. The watchdog instinct is strong in nearly every dog, so you do not need a ferocious shepherd. A yapping Pomeranian will give you plenty of warning.

If you want your dog to be a watchdog, encourage it when it barks at the door. Go to the door and praise your dog "good boy, good boy!" Barking at the door is an all-or-nothing response. You cannot expect your dog to bark only at strangers. If you try to teach it not to bark at your daughter or your neighbor, your dog will think it is not supposed to bark at anyone. The most you can expect is that your dog will learn to be quiet after the friend or family member enters the house.

Hearing-assistance dogs are trained to run to the telephone when it rings. Many hearing-impaired people have telephones with special features and flashing lights. You can train your dog to run to the flashing light by offering it praise and a food reward whenever the phone "rings." Ask a friend to call you up every ten minutes for an hour. Pick up the phone and then reward your dog. Most dogs will run to the phone for their reward after the third try.

Should I get a professionally trained guide dog, assistance dog or hearing dog?

Professionally trained dogs for handicapped people are usually retrievers or shepherds. "Seeing Eye" dogs guide sightless persons. Assistance dogs fetch objects, turn lights on and off, pull wheelchairs, and do other simple tasks. "Hearing" dogs act as alarms.

A properly trained guide dog can be obtained from one of the many training centers in the United States. Seeing Eye Dogs, Guide Dogs for the Blind, and Pilot Dogs are only three of the many non-profit associations that train dogs to guide sightless people. The dogs they use are especially selected shepherds, retrievers, and other large breeds. Consider a guide dog if you are sightless and love dogs but don't have one. Many of the associations prefer that the guide dog be the only dog in the household.

A knowledgeable trainer might be able to teach Rover to do some of the things done by an assistance dog. You might teach your own dog to pull a wheelchair if you have a little help to lead the dog while you hold the pulling leash.

Hearing-assistance dogs are of any breed, since they are intended only to sound an alarm. You don't have to buy a professionally trained hearing-assistance dog. If your daughter-in-law loves dogs and has any interest in training, she can teach Tiny to bark at the door and run to the telephone. As a matter of fact, you can teach Tiny to do that all by yourself.

Since Guide Dogs for the Blind, Hearing Dogs, Assistance Dogs," and others are all non-profit groups, most of the cost of these dogs is subsidized. If you decide on a professionally trained dog, you yourself will need several days or weeks of training to learn to use the dog.

Beware of private "trainers" who try to sell you an expensive guide dog, assistance dog, or hearing dog. Be especially cautious of a "trainer" who is not affiliated with a nationally recognized organization and who sells dogs that are "just as good" but cost thousands of dollars.

Chapter 10
When You're Not as Dexterous as You Once Were

Is the buckle on your dog's collar getting harder and harder to fasten? All of a sudden, does it take both hands to pick up the dog's water bowl to refill it at the sink? Would you rather not bend over to put your dog on its leash? Some simple techniques can make these little things easy. Some you can do yourself, some will require help to set up.

Many of these suggestions have been described in the chapters in which they are needed. You can buy all the equipment you need at hardware stores, pet stores, or order it from catalogs or on the Internet. Check the Appendix for useful sources.

Collars, leashes and tie-out chains.

Fasten your dog's collar the easy way. Get one of those adjustable nylon collars that have a two-piece plastic fastener instead of a buckle. All you have to do is push the ends of the fastener together and the collar is on tight.

Buy a tag with your name, address, and telephone number to put on your dog's collar. Most of these tags must be ordered by mail or on the Internet. Until you get your dog's tag, write your telephone number (and the word "Reward" if there is enough room) on the dog's collar with an indelible pen. Buy a light-colored nylon collar—the ink shows up better.

Put a better snap on your leash.

Does your leash have a snap that is clumsy to fasten or unfasten? Fix it with a better snap. Most hardware stores have a rack of snaps of several kinds and sizes: bolt snaps, tongue snaps, scissors snaps. Try opening and closing one of each kind and pick out the one that is the easiest for you to use. Chose a snap that is big enough for you to handle with ease. Buy a few of your choice; you'll find many uses for them. When you attach a new snap right onto the clumsy old snap, your leash will be easier to fasten and unfasten.

Don't fumble to attach a leash to the little collar ring.

Is the ring on your dog's collar hard to find or hard to grasp? This is another use for a large snap. Put the snap on the collar ring and leave it there. Now you can grab the snap and fasten the leash to the big ring at the bottom of the snap without having to fumble for the little ring on the collar. Another way is to buy a snap with a big ring on the end. Take the collar off your dog, pass the end of the collar through the ring of the snap, and put the collar back on your dog. You'll have a big, easy to use snap permanently attached to the collar.

Alternately, buy just the big ring, either a round one or a D-ring, and put the collar through this before you buckle it onto your dog. Don't use a key ring; even a medium dog can pull these apart.

Replace the snaps on your tie-out chain.

Tie out chains sold in grocery stores and pet shops come in many sizes and lengths, but they usually are fitted with a stiff tongue-type snap on each end. Use one of your better snaps on the end that you fasten to your dog. You don't have to replace the snap that came on the chain; just snap the eye of the good snap onto it, just like you did on your leash.

Use a double-snap chain.

You can get a five-foot chain with a snap on each end made up for you at most hardware stores. Hardware stores sell chain by the foot. Pick out an appropriate size of chain and a pair of easy-to use snaps with open ends. The personnel at most hardware stores will be glad to attach a snap to each end of the chain, simply by closing the open ends of the snap onto the end links of the chain.

An alternate to having a chain with a snap on each end prepared at a hardware store is to buy a short chain leash. This will have a snap on one end, a handle (usually a leather or plastic loop) on the other. Buy an open-ended snap or a double snap and have it put onto the same ring to which the handle is sewn or riveted. You can hold onto the handle when you lead your dog.

Use this chain when you walk your dog to its chain to tie it out in the yard. Attach one end of the chain to the dog's collar, lead the dog out, fasten the other end of the short chain to the tie-out chain.

If you live in a cold climate and tie your dog outside, a short chain with a snap on each end is an absolute necessity. The short chain goes in the house with the dog so the snaps never freeze.

Make it easy to use the tie-out chain.

If you can arrange it, a tie-out chain that you can reach from the door without going outside is easy to use. A hook right outside the door is a good idea to keep the end of the chain at hand.

Make your leash easy to use.

Need to put a snap on the handle end of a regular leash? Pass the loop of the handle through the eye of the snap, and then pass the rest of the leash through the loop. Pull it tight and you have a snap permanently attached to the handle. Don't do this with a short chain leash used to fasten your dog to a longer chain. The leather or plastic handle loop is not strong enough to withstand wear for very long; it will break and your dog will escape.

Is your leash too short?

Get a second leash and fasten the snap of one into the loop of the handle of the other. Now you have a double leash that's adjustable: short or long.

If you don't want to have to fasten a leash to your dog's collar, get a noose-type leash that has a ring on one end instead of a snap. Make a loop by passing the leash through the ring, and then drop the loop over your dog's head. Be more careful with a noose leash than the snap-on kind. If you aren't careful, the loop can loosen and drop off your dog. Leashes made to use in the dog show ring are usually the noose-type, but they are too short and often made of too thin material to be useful on the street.

Do you or your dog get tangled in the leash?

A retractable leash might be the answer. These leashes are available at any hardware or pet store. They come in different sizes for big and small dogs, and have a button or handle to squeeze when you want to extend or shorten the leash.

Attach your dog's leash without struggling or bending over. Is it hard for you to bend over or difficult to get the dog to hold still for the leash to be attached to its collar? A little dog training can make it easy. Establish a "attach leash" station. This should be a chair near a table where you can keep your leash and a supply of dog treats. Pick a chair from which you can reach the dog's collar with ease.

Start by sitting on the chair and calling the dog to you. When it comes, hold a treat up high and say "Rover, sit!" Give the dog the treat the instant it sits to look up at the treat. If the dog jumps around trying to get the treat, keep holding it up and saying "sit!" until it does.

Rover will learn to sit next to you after only a few attempts, because there is a food reward involved. Whenever you sit in that special chair and call, Rover will come over and sit for his treat. Then begin to prolong the interval between the time the dog sits and when it gets its treat. Gradually make it wait only as long as it takes to snap on its leash—a few seconds. If the dog gets up, wave the treat over its head and repeat "Sit!"

Soon you will be able to sit on your special chair, call the dog, attach the leash, and only then give it the treat. Remove the leash the same way: sit on your chair, tell Rover to sit, take off the leash, then give the dog a treat. Eventually you won't need the treat; you won't even need the special chair. Rover will sit for his leash to be put on or taken off while you are seated.

Immobilize your dog anywhere in the house.

Do you need to restrain your dog for grooming, cleaning eyes, ears, or applying parasite-control products? Immobilize your dog by attaching its leash to its collar, then closing the leash in any door in the house. A fabric leash works best. Don't use a chain leash for this; it's hard on the woodwork It may be necessary to tie a knot in the leash at a convenient length to keep the dog from pulling the leash out of the closed door.

Immobilize your dog in the car.

Use a fabric or nylon leash. Ask your dog to jump into the car on the passenger's side. Stay outside the car and hold onto the leash. Close the car door on the leash with you on the outside and the dog on the inside of the car.

Tie a knot in the leash on the outside of the car to prevent the dog from pulling too much of the leash into the car. (I leave a permanent knot in my "car leash" for convenience.) Tie the outside end of the leash to the door handle.

When you get out of the car, untie and take hold of the leash before you open the door to release the dog. Your dog can never escape because you are in control of its leash.

Do not use a chain leash. The chain will damage your car door. Don't use a leather leash either; leather will be weakened when the door is closed on it.

If you wish, you can purchase a harness especially made to attach your dog to a car seat belt. You can also buy a wire or fabric barrier to confine your dog to the back of a car. Most of these items are fairly easy to install and remove and may be a good option if you travel with your dog.

Filling the water bowl.

Is it difficult to pick up your dog's water bowl to refill at the sink several times a day? Refill the bowl with a houseplant watering can. You can fill the watering can at the sink and pour water into the dog's bowl without bending or stooping. You'll only need to pick up the bowl every few days to rinse it out to keep the water fresh.

Filling the food bowl.

Consider using a raised feeder if it is easier for you to fill. If the dog jumps around at feeding time, put the dog in another room, put its filled dish on the floor, then let the dog back in. If it is difficult to wash your dog's food bowl, buy a stack of inexpensive paper plates and throw the used one away every time you feed.

Get your dog the right Safe Place.

Don't buy a plastic airline-type carrier. These can be difficult to get open and closed. Before you buy a wire cage, check the way the door is held closed. A cage with a bolt closure will be easiest to use. Large cages may need to have a top and a bottom bolt to keep the door closed.

Entice your dog to enter its Safe Place with food.

Give the dog a delicious treat. Throw another treat inside the kennel and give the command "In" or "Kennel." Eventually your dog will go into its Safe Place without the treat.

See if your dog will "work" for a dog biscuit. If it won't and you need to use something more enticing, try a slice of a hotdog. If a hotdog is too messy or inconvenient, get a little foil package of cat treats at the grocery store. Very few dogs can resist the taste and smell, and you can fold over the top of the package and store the treats on a cupboard shelf.

Keeping your dog off the furniture.

Do you want to keep Rover off the white chair? Have you discovered that spray-on patented dog repellants don't work for long, electronic barriers are expensive and hard to install, mousetraps spring up and scare you but not your dog, yelling and screaming is only effective when you are in the room?

Forget the "recommended" methods. Just put something on the furniture that is uncomfortable for your dog to lie on. If you sit on the furniture routinely, use something that is easy to remove and set aside. How about a small suitcase? A pile of books? A couple of big saucepan lids? A wire letter basket? Your furniture won't be full of dog hair, you can stuff these objects in a closet when company comes, and nobody will be the wiser.

Unfortunately, a strip of aluminum foil probably won't keep your dog off the furniture. Your dog is likely just to scratch the foil into a more comfortable bed.

Chapter 11
<u>Traveling</u>

"Now that I'm retired, I want to see different places. But what should I do with Rover when I'm gone?" You've spent your entire life attending to responsibilities that keep you at home. Business, job, and family—these have limited your travels to short and infrequent trips. Now that you are retired and your family is grown, there is only Rover to prevent you from really going places. Yes, a dog is a responsibility—only you can decide if the dog's companionship is worth the trouble. When you own a dog and decide to travel, you have these four options:

> Stay home. This is not a good option. You deserve to be able to get away and have some interesting experiences.

> Give the dog away. If the dog is gone, there's nothing to tie you down, but there might not be much to come home to, either. Most of us don't consider this option acceptable. We'd rather not travel than part with our best friend.

> Take the dog along. This option is wonderful, but often impossible. Your dog may not be welcome by the people you're visiting. Your dog certainly won't be allowed if you're taking any sort of conducted tour or trip.

> Leave the dog behind. If you live with someone who is willing to care for your dog, you have the problem solved. If you live alone, leave your dog with a friend, a relative, a pet-sitter, or a boarding kennel.

Forget the first two options. Let's examine the good options to help you make the right choices.

How can I take my dog with me by automobile?

Your dog should always wear its identification tag. A tag bearing your name, address; and phone number is essential. It is your dog's ticket home if he should ever get lost. This doesn't only apply to travel by automobile, or travel by any other means. Even if you think Rover will never get away from you, get a tag, attach it firmly to a collar, put the collar on your dog, and leave it on all the time. Use a plain collar with a buckle; choke chains can come off over a dog's head. Fit the collar snug enough that the dog cannot pull out of it.

If there are no local hardware stores or pet stores that make identification tags for pets, look in the appendix and select one of the supply houses that prints the tags.

If you have a fairly large dog that has a light-colored nylon collar, you can use an indelible marker to write "REWARD" and your telephone number on the collar. That will do the job until your metal tag is mailed to you. Don't get a plastic tag; they break and fall off

Whenever your dog is riding in a car, it must always be wearing a leash. There are no exceptions to this rule. "Yes, but my dog is perfect in the car. He lies down and goes to sleep and doesn't move until we get there. Why should he wear his leash?" Many dogs ride like little ladies and gentlemen until the door is opened and they see a squirrel, another dog, or a human friend outside of the car. The best-mannered dog might jump out unexpectedly, with disastrous results. Remember, where there are cars, there is traffic. Being hit by a car is a major reason for dog fatalities. Don't take a chance that your "perfectly behaved" dog won't jump out and get hurt, lost, or killed.

How can I control my dog in the car?

How you handle your dog in your car depends on your dog's normal behavior, the type of vehicle and whether you are a passenger or the driver. These suggestions apply to short, every-day trips with your dog as well as to longer journeys.

If you are traveling in a wagon, hatchback, or SUV, one option is to place a wire dog kennel or a plastic airline carrier in the open space in the back. Once your dog is in its kennel, it is entirely secure.

In almost any vehicle except two-door sedans, you can install a wire barrier behind the front seat. The barrier keeps your dog in the back of the car, but does nothing to keep it from jumping around and barking. Some of these barriers can be installed temporarily; some are permanent and cannot easily be removed.

Pet supply catalogs and pet stores sell harnesses for dogs. Some of these have attachments to connect to human seat belts in your vehicle. Some are intended to use with a leash in place of a collar, but can be used as a seat belt by passing a belt through the harness and then connecting the belt to the seat belt fastener. In theory, if you are involved in an accident, your dog will be restrained just as is a person wearing a seat belt.

The disadvantage to confining your dog with a seat belt is

that you have to climb into the car to fasten and to release your dog. You also have to put the seat belt harness on your dog every time you take it in the car. Except for the bother, a dog seat belt is a satisfactory method of in-car restraint for your dog. Remember, your dog must also wear a collar and leash in the car so you have control of the dog when you unfasten the seat belt

How can I use the leash to control my dog in a car?

"My dog jumps around in the car. It tries to escape when I open the door. There's no place in the car that I can tie him." Many unrestrained dogs leap from window to window in a car. Many dogs try to make a dash for freedom any time a car door is opened. If Rover is properly restrained in your car, he can't jump around. If Rover is still restrained when you open the door, he can't escape. Solve theses problems quickly and easily. Here's how to do it:

> Get a fabric leash at least four feet long. You might prefer to keep this leash exclusively for restraining Rover in the car. You will close this leash in the car door to immobilize your dog. Most dogs will need about 2 ½ feet of leash freedom inside the car. You can experiment and adjust the inside portion of the leash to whatever length restrains your dog the best.

> Tie a large knot in the leash 2 ½ feet from the snap end. Tie two or more knots together to make a really bulky knot. When you close the car door on the leash, the knot will be outside the car. The purpose of the knot is to keep Rover from pulling the leash into the car. The doors of some cars fit tightly enough to make this impossible, but tie the knot anyway, just in case.

> Snap the leash onto Rover's collar and let him jump into either the back seat or the passenger's front seat, wherever you prefer him to ride. If you are driving a van, Rover can ride in the passenger's seat or behind the front seats. If you have a SUV or similar vehicle with a tailgate, Rover can ride back there if you like.

> Close the door on the leash so that the knot and the free end of the leash including the hand loop are outside of the car. Rover is restrained by the short length of the leash that is inside the car.

> Walk around and enter the car from the driver's door or the other side door. When you get out of the car, use any door except the one closed on the leash. Walk around and grab the outside end of the leash before you open the door. Rover can never escape because you are always holding his leash.

Use a leash made of nylon or cotton web to close in the door of your car. In an emergency, you can use a length of clothesline with a snap tied onto one end. If you use a chain, it will damage the edge of the car door. If you close the car door on a leather leash a few times, the leather may be weakened enough to break.

When your dog is in the car and confined by the leash, you'll have several feet of leash hanging outside the car. With older model cars, you were able to tie the leash to the door handle so it didn't blow around as you drive. Most new vehicles have recessed door handles that make this impossible, so you can tie the leash into a small bundle and just let it hang there outside the car.

If you prefer, you can use a retractable leash to confine your dog in the car. Lock the leash, leaving only two or three feet of length between the handle and the dog. Close the car door on the leash, leaving the handle on the outside of the car. When you let the dog out, grab the handle before you open the car door.

Even if you are confining your dog with a wire barrier or a dog crate in your vehicle, keep your leash or rope attached to the dog's collar at all times. Take hold of the end of the leash before you release the dog. If your dog chews leashes, use a chain as the part inside the crate or behind the barrier. Attach another leash or a piece of rope to the end of the chain to take hold of before you release your dog from the car.

My dog gets car sick.

Car sickness in dogs is quite common. The dog rides for a while before it starts to pant or yawn, then it vomits. Individual dogs vary in the length of time they can ride before becoming sick.

Take Rover for short rides when his stomach is empty. Start with a five-minute cruise. To allow your dog to get used to the motion, gradually increase the length of your trip for the next dozen outings.

Most dogs that spend enough time in a moving car get over the tendency to get carsick. Some dogs never do, and some dogs will always get sick if they ride after a meal. If your dog is one that routinely vomits in the car, you can give it the same anti-nausea medication that humans use. A medium or big dog, 40 pounds or more, gets an adult human dose. A small dog, less than 40 pounds, gets half a human dose. Don't use the medication for toy breeds; the tablets cannot be divided into small enough doses for really tiny dogs.

My dog barks at everything outside the car.

Most dogs won't bark when they are prevented from jumping around in a car. If your dog still barks when properly restrained, use the anti-bark collar to solve the problem.

My dog is afraid of the car. He won't jump in.

If your dog is small enough to lift, put your car leash on your dog, put him in the car and give him a treat. Don't close the door or drive off. Let the dog jump out or lift him out. Wait a minute, lift him in again, and give him another treat. Do this three or four times a day for a few days before you actually drive with the dog in the car.

If your dog is not small enough for you to lift easily, put your car leash on him, lead him to the car door, and give him a treat. I he is really afraid, you might have to do this quite a few times, even quite a few days, before he will willingly approach the car.

When your dog comes to the car door without fear, hold the treat inside the car and make him reach for it. When he responds, say "in" and give him the treat. You can also get into the car first, sit on the seat, and coax the dog to jump in with you. A little tugging on the leash while you show him the treat will help.

Most dogs that won't readily jump into the car are not really afraid. They just need a little coaxing to learn what is expected of them.

Be careful when you leave your dog alone in the car. Every summer, newspapers are full of horror stories about children and animals suffering and even dying from heat exposure when left in closed cars. If parked in the sun on a hot day, your dog can suffer from the heat even if the windows are open. Be careful that you never leave Rover to suffocate in a hot car. Better to get your lunch at a drive-through and park somewhere shady while you eat it.

If you find that you have to leave your dog alone in a car, it is wise to raise the windows enough so that the locks cannot be reached from the outside, and to lock the doors. Dog thieves exist, but pranksters are more common. Some misguided person may decide to release your "poor" dog from confinement.

What should I take in the car for Rover?

If you're just going to the groomer or to visit a friend, you don't need to take anything for Rover's comfort. If you're going on an all-day trip, take along a bottle of water and a bowl to offer your dog a drink occasionally, especially in the summer time.

Food: For day trips, it is best to feed Rover when you get home. That way you won't have to stop to exercise the dog or take the risk that it will eliminate in the car. If you are going on an extended trip, take a supply of the dog's usual food. Don't forget a can opener if you're feeding canned food. You need only one bowl—feed the dog, rinse out the bowl, and then use the bowl for water.

Vaccination certificates: If you are traveling abroad, be sure you take along your vaccination certificates. It's a good idea to take the certificates even if you're not leaving the country. If you have to board your dog during your trip, you'll need proof that it was vaccinated.

Medication: If Rover is on any sort of medication, or if you are going to be traveling when Rover gets his monthly heartworm or parasite control products, be sure to take the medication with you.

Clean-up equipment: Don't forget your Pooper Scooper and disposable bags to clean up if you must exercise Rover in a public place.

Should I make advance arrangements for Rover?

If you are planning to stop at a hotel or a motel, call ahead and find out if dogs are permitted in the rooms. Often dogs are not permitted, because of the potential for causing damage, disturbing other guests with their barking, and leaving fleas (or stools) on the premises.

"Can Rover stay in the car?" Yes, weather permitting, if you can trust him not to damage anything or bark at night. If you leave your dog alone overnight in a vehicle, lengthen its leash inside the car so that it can move around relatively freely. Leave a bowl of water on the floor within the dog's reach. If your dog is a barker in the yard, he'll probably bark when he's alone in the car; take along your bark collar and avoid complaints.

CODY

Be careful. If you're not sure about your dog's deportment, make plans other than to leave him alone in a vehicle. I learned this the hard way.

Cody, one of my best field trial Labradors, was a well-trained and well-behaved six-year-old who preferred to ride in the front seat of my truck than in his kennel in the back. When I had to bring an extra dog home from a field trial, I gave the new dog his kennel and let Cody ride in front.

We stopped for lunch. Before I could choke down a Big Mac and fries, Cody had shredded the truck upholstery and put a few teeth marks on the steering wheel. He was perfect when I was with him, but a different dog when he was alone.

Can I take Rover on a bus?

If you're traveling by bus, Rover will have to stay home. All animals are on the prohibited baggage list of all major bus companies. Nor are animals permitted to ride with their owners, even if they are in secure carriers

Can Rover fly with me?

If you are flying to your destination, Rover can go with you under some circumstances. If your flight is much more than six hours long, I would recommend that Rover stay home. Six hours in a closed carrier is long enough for any animal. If you have to change planes in major airports, it is wise to ask the attendant to check that your dog will be on your next flight.

Taking your dog with you on an airplane requires planning in advance with the airline. Most airlines restrict the number of animals that can be taken on each flight, so you'll have to contact the booking agent well ahead of your intended trip.

Your dog must be transported in an approved airline animal carrier. Fortunately, these kennels are easy to obtain and relatively inexpensive, except for the huge ones for very large dogs. It may be possible to rent an appropriate kennel from the airline. It might be possible to borrow, buy, or rent a carrier from your local humane society—they get many donations of carriers when dog owners are through with them. It's worth while to call the local humane society and inquire. It may be possible to use the regular kennel you use to transport your dog in your van or car. The advantage of this is that Rover will be already accustomed to going places in his kennel and will feel more comfortable.

Approved kennels or carriers are made of plastic, with doors of metal bars and metal guards over the ventilation areas on the sides. You can buy these kennels at pet stores, some hardware or feed stores, and from dog supply catalogs. Airlines do not allow dogs to be transported in wire crates. The kennel should only be big enough for the dog to stand up and turn around in. If the kennel is oversized or very heavy, you probably will be required to pay an extra fee.

Remember your current health certificate and proof of rabies vaccine. No airline will accept your dog without them. The certificates will be taped in an envelope to the dog's kennel.

The airline will tell you when and where to check in your dog in its kennel. Often the dog will go with your regular baggage. Since the dog will be in the baggage compartment, the outdoor temperature determines if it will be safe on the plane. Baggage compartments are neither heated nor air-conditioned, and your dog will be taken on a cart from the airport building to the plane. Overheating is a greater threat than chilling, especially for long-haired or short-nosed dogs. Most airlines will refuse to transport animals if the weather is dangerously hot.

If your dog is very small and can be transported in a carrier that will fit under an airline seat, you may be able to carry the dog aboard. You must plan ahead—the airline limits the number of animals allowed under seats, usually to one per flight. Don't try to smuggle tiny little Rover onto the plane. You might find that both you and Rover are removed from the flight in a most inconvenient place.

If you are taking Rover on a commuter flight that is less than two hours long, it pays to call and ask if the rules are different. I have been allowed to take a small dog in its carrier in the isle of the plane on very short trips. You still will need your rabies and health certificates to be allowed to board with an animal.

Can Rover go with me in a motor home or travel trailer?

If you travel in a mobile home or trailer, your dog is in luck. It can go with you just as any other member of the family. It is a good idea to take a portable Safe Place in the mobile home, so Rover can be confined when you leave the vehicle.

Be sure that you take Rover's usual dog food and medication. You may need Rover's tie-out chain and a ground anchor to use at a campground.

Before you finalize your travel plans, check to see which campgrounds allow dogs. Most do, but don't take a chance that you will be rejected because you have a dog. Don't forget health and rabies certificates, especially if you are traveling abroad.

How can I leave my dog at home?

If you're lucky enough to live with someone who will care for Rover in your absence, you are in the fortunate minority. Be sure you provide enough dog food and other supplies to care for your dog in your absence, and bring back a really nice present for the caretaker.

More often you live alone or your companions want to travel with you. Other arrangements must be made for Rover. There are several possibilities for you to explore:

> Find a friend or relative that will keep Rover at her house while you are away

If you are going on an extended trip, this will have to be a good friend indeed, as well as a real dog lover. This friend deserves a really special gift when you return.

> If it is impossible or inconvenient for any of your friends

or relatives to keep Rover at their homes, ask if they will come to your house at least twice a day to feed and exercise your dog. This is a good option if you have trustworthy friends.

> Find a person who boards only a few dogs at a time in her home. This arrangement will offer Rover much more individual attention than will a big commercial kennel. The best way to locate such a person is to ask your dog-owning friends and your veterinarian's office personnel. Seldom do in-home boarders advertise in the yellow pages.

> Locate a pet sitting service that will come to your house at least twice a day to take care of Rover and to water your plants. You may be able to hire a high school or college student that is a relative or a relative of a friend and needs some extra money. To locate a professional pet-sitting service, look in the yellow pages of your phone book for pet sitting services or kennels. Your veterinarian's office staff may be able to suggest people who provide these services. Remember to ask for references before you hire someone.

Even if you are hiring a person who is not a professional pet sitter, call a professional to ask what he charges for his services by the day or week. That way, you can get some idea of what you should offer your amateur sitter.

> Persuade or hire someone to stay at your house while you are gone. There are professional pet sitters who offer this service, or you may be able to hire a college student for the job. You'll probably have to stock the refrigerator and the freezer for him or her, but Rover, your mail, and your houseplants will appreciate being cared for in their own environment.

Before you hire anyone, be sure that you know and trust the person who will have access to your home and all your possessions. The advantage of hiring professionals is that they will be bonded and insured.

Leaving your dog at a commercial kennel.

Rover will like this option the least. He'd rather stay in his own home, even in someone else's home while you are away. In a boarding kennel, your dog will be confined to a cage or run, will hear and smell many unfamiliar dogs, and will probably be offered a different diet than he is accustomed to eat. Even in the best boarding kennel, your dog will miss your individual attention and affection. All dogs, even the most happy and outgoing dog will experience a significant amount of stress in a boarding kennel. However, often there is no other option. Rover stays in a kennel or you can't travel. Don't feel guilty about this; life isn't perfect for any of us.

Boarding kennels are not all alike. Some are luxurious, some are adequate, and some are decidedly below standard for the industry. It is important to pick a kennel that will give Rover the best possible care while you are away.

Running a boarding kennel is hard work. A boarding kennel is a time-consuming, difficult business. Establishing a boarding kennel requires a large monetary investment. If you think it's just putting a dog in a cage and taking the owner's money, consider how you'd cope with caring for, cleaning up after, feeding, medicating, and listening to the barking of up to a hundred dogs a day. When you judge the quality of a boarding kennel, try to determine the level of care that the boarders receive, not the elaborateness of the décor.

If possible, get references from other dog owners who have used the kennel. Always ask the opinion of the personnel at one or more veterinary hospitals in the area in which the kennel is located. They will be the first to hear if their clients have had unfavorable experiences with the kennel. Area veterinary hospitals also will be the ones to treat any dogs that need medical attention while they are boarding. They will know if the kennel is or is not vigilant about their boarders' health.

Every boarding kennel will require proof of vaccinations against the major viral and bacterial diseases of dogs. Not only do the vaccinations protect Rover, but requiring proof gives you the assurance that the other dogs in the kennel are vaccinated also. Don't forget to take your certificates when you take Rover to the kennel. Check the certificates well ahead of the boarding date, in case Rover is due for a booster.

Kennel operators hear this all the time "I want to look at the place my dog will be staying." It is quite normal for you to want to examine the facilities in which Rover will be confined while boarding, but not all kennel operators will allow you to do this. Look at it from their perspective; they have a routine for cleaning, exercising, and feeding. The boarding dogs get used to the routine and to the presence of the regular personnel. A stranger in the kennel is very disturbing; strangers cause all the dogs to jump around and bark, scattering food and upsetting water bowls. Some kennel operators will allow you to look at the facilities only at certain times. Others will allow you to peek in a window. Some will conduct you through the kennel and tolerate the disturbance, but be understanding if they won't.

One way to judge a kennel, even if it is after the fact, is that Rover should come back to you in normal weight, happy, and clean. If you are gone more than a week and Rover is not eating well, he'll be notably thinner. If Rover is on a special diet, or if he is a particularly picky eater, plan to take his regular food along. Take enough of his favorite canned food to last for his stay. If Rover only eats fresh food, ask if you can bring the food frozen in one-serving portions and put it in a freezer in the kennel.

Don't expect a break in the boarding fee if you provide Rover's meals. It's a lot more trouble to serve a dog a special diet, even if provided by the owner, than to feed it the kennel's regular food. Of course, if Rover is on some medication, or if his regularly administered heartworm or parasite control is due to be given while he is at the kennel, be sure to provide the medication, labeled and with written instructions. I have never heard of a kennel that charged an extra fee for administering even daily medication to a dog that needed it, but it is a possibility.

If Rover has been in a state of fear for his entire stay, he won't act like his usual happy self for days after he gets home. If the kennel employees don't keep the dogs' quarters clean, Rover will come back dirty and smelly. Some dogs will get dirty even if the kennel is cleaned very regularly; since they are in a strange place, the dogs might mess in their runs and tramp around in the mess. Many kennels ask owners to let them know when they are taking their dogs home so they can bathe the dogs before they go.

If your travels involve leaving or returning on a Sunday or holiday, ask what the kennels' hours are on those days. Often the kennel is closed, except for routine caring for the dogs, and will accept or release boarders only the day before or the day after.

Almost all kennels require reservations be made in advance. Remember, holidays and the summer vacation months are kennels' busy time. If you are traveling during that period, make Rover's reservation long in advance, or you might find that the kennel of your choice is filled.

Boarding kennels usually calculate their charges by the number of days your dog will be staying. Occasionally some kennels will offer a weekly or monthly rate, if you're taking a long trip. Even though the cost of a boarding kennel is not inconsiderable, it probably will be less than half of the expense of hiring a full-time house sitter.

Whenever you leave your dog in the care of others, designate someone to make decisions about Rover in your absence. Be sure that the caretaker has the name and telephone number of this person. It is unlikely but possible that Rover could need medical intervention or some other treatment that the caretaker is not authorized to provide. Name a good friend, a relative, or even your veterinarian (ask first) to contact if the need arises. If possible, leave a telephone number at your destination so you can be reached in an emergency.

Chapter 12
Living Arrangements

"Mom, you can't keep up this big place by yourself any longer. You'll just have to come live with us."

"I have to find another apartment. This one has too many stairs."

"This building has been sold and the new owners won't allow dogs."

"Dad, it's time you start thinking about a retirement community."

So many things can happen. When lifestyle changes are unavoidable, what happens to Rover? The ideal solution is to take Rover with you. In many situations, this is not easy to do. You might have the following concerns:

> How can I convince my daughter that Rover won't make her house dirty? That he won't destroy anything? That he won't bark all the time?

> My adult children have a dog of their own. How can I convince my son that two dogs are not too much?

> My daughter-in-law never had a dog. She doesn't think she wants one.

The solution to these problems is the correct use of your dog's Safe Place. You originally established a Safe Place for Rover to keep him out of trouble when you were not present to supervise his actions. As soon as Rover became reliable in the house when he was alone, you probably confined him in his Safe Place only when you had visitors who didn't like dogs.

Even though you seldom use it, it is time to reinstate Rover's Safe Place if you must live with someone who is not enthusiastic about accepting your dog. If you can demonstrate that Rover will never be loose alone in the house to make a mess, damage anything, bite the kids, or get away, you'll have a good chance to convince your family that Rover should stay.

This will be easy if Rover is a relatively small dog and his Safe Place is an easily moveable wire cage. You could put the cage in your new bedroom. You could put the cage in the hallway. You could even put the cage in the basement if Rover doesn't have to stay in it too often or for too long a time.

Even if Rover is too large for a bedroom-sized wire cage, or if he has been accustomed to a small room as his Safe Place, you probably can establish a new Safe Place for him. Discuss the situation with the family. Select a room or a location and modify it to safely confine your dog. Buy a door barrier or a huge wire cage. If your family is concerned about your comfort and happiness, they will be anxious to help.

Remember, if you made a promise to keep your dog safely in his Safe Place whenever you are not supervising him, you are absolutely obliged to keep your promise. No "just going down to the corner" and leaving Rover loose in the house. No falling asleep while watching television when Rover is not confined.

If the family welcomes my dog, does it still need a Safe Place?

A Safe Place for your dog is a very good idea even if your adult children say, "sure, brings Rover. We'd love to have him." It will take Rover at least a few weeks to get used to the new routine. Don't take the chance that Rover will miss his usual elimination time and make a mess in the house. Eliminate the possibility that Rover will decide that children's toys are something good to chew. Don't allow your dog to jeopardize his welcome. The family that is happy to have your dog may present you with some new problems. For example, you may have to insist that Rover not be fed too many treats or be allowed to ignore his discipline. However, your grandchildren may just love to take your dog for walks and give Rover lots of exercise. You can walk with the dog when the kids are in school.

I must move to a smaller house or another apartment. Where will I find a rental that will allow my dog?

I'm sure you've seen the many, many ads in the local newspapers that describe just the new dwelling you need and want, but that end with the statement "no pets." We tend to be critical of property owners who refuse to allow a dog or a cat, but landlords have learned from bad experiences.

Many renters demonstrate absolutely no regard for the owners' property. Apartments that are carpeted or that are rented furnished are the most likely not to allow animals because of the damage done by the pets of careless renters. It seldom is successful to try to convince a property owner that Rover is quite, clean, and harmless. What can you do if you find an acceptable place, but Rover is not welcomed?

You could look for another place or you could find Rover another home. Let's forget that last option; Rover stays.

TED

When I was attending college, I lived in some really small and inconvenient apartments just so I could keep my dogs. The bedroom of one apartment was so small that there simply was no space for my German shepherd puppy's cage. I solved the problem by scrapping the bedside table and putting the large cage in its place. I put a piece of plywood on top of the cage and used it like a table to hold my lamp, telephone, and books. Ted, the puppy, slept next to me in safe confinement, and was safe and comfortable while I attended classes. This solution wouldn't suit an interior decorator, but it worked very well for both me and my puppy.

How do I find a dog-friendly dwelling?

It's a renters' market out there. In most locations, there are more apartments to rent than there are people to rent them. There are few owners who allow pets with no restrictions, but there are many who allow pets but impose some regulations on the kind, size, and number of animals that live in each unit.

Many apartments charge a small addition to the monthly rent or lease to include a pet. If the amount is not excessive, that could be a satisfactory solution. Most apartments that allow pets ask for a one-time damage deposit to be refunded at the end of the rental or lease period if the animal has not damaged the premises. This is a perfectly legitimate request.

Some rentals allow only dogs below a certain size or weight.

You'll have to find a place that fits Rover. Almost all rental properties require the tenants to clean up their dog's waste on the premises, but you've always done that anyway. Rentals usually have the authority to reject dogs that bark and annoy other tenants; you still have your no-bark collar and can eliminate that problem.

Don't try to sneak Rover into a rental that doesn't allow dogs. Sooner or later you are sure to be discovered and have to give up your dog or have to move again.

My apartment is not going to allow dogs anymore.

Call your lawyer. If you don't have a lawyer, call the legal aid society. It is very likely that a lawyer can find a "grandfather clause" that will allow tenants to keep the dogs that already live with them, but will not allow any new dogs in the building. You or your lawyer need not be belligerent about it—in most cases a simple request will do.

I must move to a retirement community.

Except for the age of the residents, most retirement communities are very much like ordinary condominiums, they consist of individual apartments, each with one or more bedrooms, a kitchen, a living room, often a garage for your car, and sometimes even a small yard for each unit. A retirement community differs because of the many services that are offered to their senior residents. These services may include catered meals, a restaurant, house cleaning, transportation, a gymnasium or physical therapy appropriate for senior residents, and even a swimming pool.

Almost all retirement communities allow pets on a limited basis. There may be a restriction on the size or number of the pets, usually one pet to a unit, and often limited to small or medium dogs. Often there are rules about where residents can walk their dogs. Some communities charge a one-time or monthly pet fee, just as do pet-friendly rental apartments. If you find a retirement community that won't allow you to keep Rover, look for another one. Because of the services offered, retirement communities are significantly more costly than are rental apartments and must cater to the desires of their residents.

I must move to an assisted-living facility.

Assisted-living facilities provide care for handicapped or otherwise impaired people who need help with daily activities. Most facilities of this type provide only a bedroom and a bathroom or a small apartment for each resident, and communal eating and activity areas for groups.

Residents of many assisted-living facilities are not allowed to keep their own dogs. These facilities often have a dog or two that circulate among the dog-loving residents. Unless you can persuade the personnel that your dog would be just perfect for this job, I'm afraid that Rover will need a new home.

Part IV: Some Dog Problems Have Difficult Solutions

Chapter 13
When There Are No Options

Let's face it. There will be situations that make it impossible for you to keep your dog. Some of these situations will arise because of problems of your own; some because of problems caused by your dog's health or behavior. What are these situations and how can we minimize the stress and trauma both to you and your dog?

I am no longer physically able to care for my dog.

Not being able to care for your dog doesn't mean that it is merely inconvenient to care for your dog, even though some people will try to tell you differently. Maybe you'd rather stay in bed longer in the morning, maybe you'd prefer not to take the dog out, but if you can physically care for your dog, you and you alone should have the choice of keeping it or parting with it.

If you simply can't manage the daily care of your dog and you don't live with anyone willing or capable of helping, you must face giving up your dog. It is better to part with a dog than it is to neglect it.

My living arrangements cannot include my dog.

Changes in your living arrangements could make it impossible to keep your dog. You might find yourself living with relatives or other people who not only don't welcome Rover, but won't tolerate him. We dog lovers deplore this situation, but it exists. Many rental properties forbid pets, and for good reason. Tenants are notoriously careless about pets' damage. Some rentals allow dogs but require a "damage deposit" or an increase in the monthly rental to cover repairs caused by the pet. If you find yourself in a nursing home, it is unlikely that your dog will be permitted.

What if my dog is very old or sick?

Old age is not a disease. Blindness and deafness are not death sentences. Lameness within reason isn't a death sentence either. These conditions require adjustments on the part of both you and your dog, but by themselves, they are not valid indications to end the life of your dog. Dogs need not be euthanized for trivial complaints. Think of it this way. What would you do if you had the same condition? You'd want to keep on living.

As with human health conditions, many canine medical problems can be handled, if not cured, with appropriate treatment and sometimes surgery. Yes, the cost of some of the procedures can be prohibitive. Help with your dog's medical expenses sometimes can be had from a humane society or a breed rescue group. Some suggestions for locating this help can be found in the Appendix.

Untreatable pain, terminal organ malfunction, and serious loss of mental ability are conditions that make it unlikely that Rover has any quality time left. If your old friend is suffering, you know what you must ask your veterinarian to do for him.

CHIP

Veterinarians occasionally get clients who are just seeking a second opinion. John Franklin was one of those. Chip, his ten-year-old chocolate Labrador, was limping badly on his left hind leg. "When did this start?" I asked Mr. Franklin.

"Three days ago. I try to give him some exercise every day. He loves to retrieve a Frisbee, so I throw it for him for a few minutes. Wednesday, he came back with the Frisbee but he was walking on three legs."

I waited for the rest of the story. Mr. Franklin was obviously very unhappy. "Yesterday, I took Chip to his regular vet." Mr. Franklin named a well-known colleague of mine. "He said that Chip would have to have surgery to fix his leg. Without the surgery, Chip would have to be put to sleep. When he told me what it would cost, I about passed out. I'm barely making it on Social Security."

I asked, "What did the other doctor say was the matter with Chip's leg?"

"Something about his knee. I didn't even know that dogs had knees. He said it was like a football injury, that Chip's knee moved like a drawer—I didn't understand that at all."

"Let's get Chip up on the table, and I'll take a look," I said. What I really meant was that I'd take a feel. Unless the dog was walking, both hind legs looked exactly alike.

I called the technician, and between the three of us, we wrestled Chip up onto the examining table. I palpated the dog's leg.

"Look here," I placed Mr. Franklin's hand on the dog's stifle joint so he could feel it. I moved the joint backward and forward a little. "That's called an anterior drawer movement because the bones that are supposed to be fixed tightly together move back and forth like a drawer. Chip has a partial rupture of a cruciate ligament."

"That's just what the other doctor said! I couldn't remember the exact words. I can never afford that surgery. Can't it be fixed any other way? Do I have to have Chip put to sleep?"

"Well, Mr. Franklin, to make his leg as good as new, surgery is the only option. The surgery would have to be done by a specialist and not only would it be expensive, but after the surgery Chip would have to be confined so that he could not run and jump while he recovered."

Mr. Franklin's face fell. "So that's it? You'll put him to sleep then?"

"Certainly not!" Diplomacy is not my strong suite, but I wanted to make myself clear. "Chip is your pet. Just because his leg won't be perfect, it doesn't mean he has to die. If we treat him properly, Chip might always limp a little but he won't be in real pain. He'll get around much better than a person who uses a cane, because he has four legs to walk on, not just two."

Mr. Franklin smiled for the first time. "What do you have to do to help him? Can I afford it?"

Like his dog, Chip's owner was quite plump, so more diplomacy was indicated. I said, "Actually, Mr. Franklin, you might save some money—on dog food." I turned on the weighing function of the examining table. "Look here, Chip weighs 89 pounds."

"What should he weigh?"

"About 70 pounds at the most. His weight is at least partly the cause of his problem." I went on to explain about getting Chip to a normal weight by proper feeding and helping Chip's leg by limiting his exercise to leash walking for the next month or two. I dispensed some mild pain medication in case the dog seemed very uncomfortable. The secretary made appointment to have Chip weighed again in three weeks.

As Mr. Franklin led Chip out of the examining room, each of them was limping a little. Well, I thought, nobody has to be perfect to enjoy life.

My dog is a dangerous biter.

Nobody should be afraid of his own dog. If you can't handle your dog safely, you certainly can't consider it to be your best friend. This does not include a dog that is ordinarily a good pet. The dog that might resist, growl, or even snap under special circumstances such as taking away its food or cutting its toenails is not a danger to you. It's the dog that will bite if you reach down to fasten its leash, the dog that you can't tell to get off the couch, the dog that you are afraid even to lay a hand on—this is the animal that you should not keep.

The dog that might bite strangers who enter your house is just being a watchdog. A senior with a dependable watchdog may actually be safer than a senior without one, but you certainly don't want Rover to bite your friends. The solution to this problem is so simple that it really doesn't need discussion. When your friends come to visit, put Rover in the back room.

What happens to my dog if I give it up?

"I'll find it a good home." That will take a lot of effort and luck. Presuming that the dog is in relatively good health and relatively well mannered, first try your relatives and friends. You might be one of the lucky few that finds someone who would love to have Rover.

When you've talked to all your relatives and friends and nobody wants or needs another dog, try calling your veterinarian's office. Ask the secretary to make a note of your dilemma "Mrs. Smith's dog Rover needs a new home." Maybe the office has a bulletin board with notices of dogs wanted and homes wanted. Just maybe someone will be looking for a dog just like Rover.

If Rover is a purebred dog, or even mostly one breed, you should try the local and national breed rescue groups. They can be found on the Internet. Ask for whippet rescue for example. If you're lucky, there will be a rescue group near you, or at least one that is willing to take Rover if you transport him. You could call dog breeders in your area; none of them are likely to want Rover themselves but they may know someone who would like an adult dog of that breed.

Consider a humane society. With the national trend toward "No-Kill" societies, this might not be as bad as it sounds. Private (non-government supported) shelters don't kill healthy, friendly dogs. Most of the shelters don't even kill some dogs with medical problems; they treat the problem or try to get a home that can deal with it.

Ask about the policies of the local shelters by visiting them or asking questions on the telephone. Private humane societies are not obliged to accept all dogs, so they might refuse Rover or put him on a waiting list for admittance.

The dog warden is absolutely the last person to call for a new home for Rover. If dogs are not purchased within a certain number of days, most wardens are required to euthanize them.

Placing an advertisement in the newspaper, "free to good home," is a risky idea. You never know who will answer, and what will become of any dog that is "free." Will the recipients decide that they don't really want Rover and dump him somewhere? After all, he didn't cost them a thing. Some people advocate charging a nominal sum for Rover under the theory that a person who has paid for a dog is more likely to value it. In reality, a dog that is no longer a puppy or has no other outstanding features is unlikely to attract a buyer.

If you are parting with Rover because the dog is an unacceptable biter, you have very few options. Nobody will knowingly take a biter; no humane society will accept a biter for placement, no dog warden will sell a dangerous biter to an uninformed person. Vicious biters, I'm afraid, must be euthanized. You can have your veterinarian do it, pay for it, and pay for the disposition of the body. You can have the dog taken to a warden who is obliged to take all relinquished dogs, tell him the truth, and he'll take care of the whole thing. If it is any consolation to you, in most states, people who perform euthanasia on animals are required to have training to do it correctly and painlessly.

Chapter 14
<u>Euthanasia: Why? When? How?</u>

I'll bet you would like to skip reading this chapter. I don't blame you; this is a terribly depressing subject. But the sad reality is that "having the dog put to sleep" is one of the common ways that senior citizens lose their canine companions. Many of you will be faced with the problem of terminating the lives of your dogs some day. Perhaps the issue won't be so painful if you know some facts well in advance of the event.

There are many reasons offered by relatives, friends, and even by owners themselves for euthanizing their dogs. Some of these reasons are valid, but some are not.

Old age is not a disease.

Every creature that lives a long life gets old. None of us is a "puppy" any more, but that doesn't mean that we are ready to die. We are just less frisky than we used to be, slower moving and more likely to take it easy.

"You have to get rid of that dog; it's too old and can hardly get around." How many times have seniors heard that one from friends or relatives? It's amazing how well meaning people will presume to tell the elderly what decisions to make about the lives of their dogs. They listen to your opinions and then say, "Yes, but…" Don't listen to this. You and only you have the right and the ability to make decisions about your dog.

Your old dog may be arthritic and lame, have poor vision, poor hearing, and not seem very responsive anymore. But if you had those problems, would you be at the end of your life? Probably not.

We humans see our doctors for help with our age-related infirmities. We take medication to alleviate pain and to help prevent or control some of the effects of aging on our bodies. We might have to undergo surgery to remove growths or to correct organ malfunctions. Modern veterinary medicine offers most of these remedies to dogs as well.

"Yes, but the vet costs too much." That's another "yes, but" often heard by seniors. It all depends on what you consider "too much." If it means that you can't buy your own medication, then it is too much. If it means that you don't take that vacation, it probably isn't too much. If it means saving the life of your valued friend, a lot of money may not be too much.

You have several options when you are faced with large veterinary bills. First, discuss the issue frankly with your veterinarian. Animal doctors are not in the business to kill; they are there to help. Almost all veterinarians will make every effort to help senior citizens keep their dogs.

It is never wrong to ask your veterinarian about the cost of any medical procedure before you consent to having it done for your dog. It is never wrong to ask if a procedure is absolutely necessary for diagnosis or treatment. It is never wrong to ask what is likely to be the outcome if a procedure is not done. It certainly is not wrong to tell a veterinarian that you can't deal with extremely expensive medical intervention, and to ask if there is a less-expensive option or if there is any available financial help. If you want to, it is never wrong to seek a second opinion from another veterinarian. Most important, it is never right to feel like a tightwad or an uncaring owner if you simply don't have the money.

"Yes, but it makes the house dirty." This is another "reason" for the euthanasia of a senior's dog. Incontinence, both of urine and feces, is a commonplace situation in old age of many species, humans and dogs included. In some instances, a veterinarian can suggest medication or diet that will minimize, if not eliminate, the problem. In other instances, the best medical treatment in the world can't prevent the condition.

Please realize that your dog isn't purposely messing in the wrong place; it simply can't help itself any longer. You and only you can decide if your dog should die for its unwilling infractions. Don't listen to Aunt Tillie when she says she'd never have that dog in her house. After all, it's your house, not Aunt Tillie's.

How can you manage an incontinent dog and still have a reasonably sanitary, odor-free home? You need an un-carpeted, large, comfortable confinement area for the dog, a couple of old blankets, a washer and a dryer, and a stack of newspapers. And, of course, you must have the dedication and the willingness to go to some trouble to keep your best friend.

With that list in mind, it's obvious how you can care for an incontinent dog. Spread newspapers in the dog's area, cover the papers with a blanket, and change the papers and wash and dry the blanket as necessary. If the dog is incontinent in its sleep, you might have to sponge it off or bathe it occasionally. When faced with the decision of life or death for your dog, it is worth a few days or weeks of effort before you decide to have it euthanized.

"Yes, but it's blind." Lack of vision is a relatively easy handicap for a dog owner to deal with. Just don't move the furniture and don't let your dog out without a fenced yard or on a leash. You will be surprised at how well your dog gets along in its familiar environment with relatively little sight or no sight at all.

"Yes, but it can't hear." Lack of hearing is even less of a handicap than is lack of vision to a dog. You will have to touch your deaf dog to get its attention, and you will have to use hand motions to indicate your intentions to the dog. If teaching a dog to obey hand singles sound difficult, consider this: stand in front of the dog and make whatever gesture you choose for "come" with a piece of food in your hand. Then give the dog the treat. After you have done that only a few times, the dog will associate the gesture with the food, and the food with coming to you to get it. You have trained your dog to obey a hand signal.

How do I judge my dog's quality of life?

In our present society, humans do a lot of suffering from intractable pain and debility. Humans are sometimes maintained on life-support systems long after they have absolutely no hope of even partial recovery. For humans, voluntary termination of life is not usually considered to be an option. In this regard, it is better to be a dog. When it is absolutely necessary, you can end your dog's suffering quickly, painlessly, and legally.

How will you know when the time has come? Don't press your veterinarian for the answer. If he or she recommends euthanasia and you have your doubts, you may find yourself blaming the veterinarian unreasonably for "killing" your dog. When is euthanasia really needed?

> When your dog is incapacitated. When it can't rise without crying in pain in spite of receiving appropriate medication. When it can't walk; when it can't eat.

> When your dog has inoperable malignancies of major structures or rapidly spreading malignancies that cannot be controlled by medical or surgical means.

> When your dog has failure of major organs, such as end-stage kidney disease, non-responsive congestive heart failure, terminal liver disease.

> If your dog is a really dangerous biter. Even though such a dog may be physically healthy, it is not mentally healthy. It is irresponsible to place a biting dog in another home where it may injure a person or another animal.

Ask your veterinarian's advise, but make your own decisions. When you see that your dog has no good quality of life remaining, you will know that it is time to do the merciful thing and say goodbye to your old friend.

How is euthanasia carried out?

Humane euthanasia of dogs is properly done only by a veterinarian and only by the administration of an intravenous lethal injection. In most instances, the dog to be euthanized is brought into the veterinarian's office for the procedure. A few veterinarians will come to the owner's house to carry out euthanasia.

Some veterinarians recommend the injection of a potent tranquilizer before the euthanasia solution is given. Tranquilizers can be injected into a muscle, but lethal drugs must always be given in a vein. A dog that is tranquilized beforehand is unlikely to resist the manipulation required to insert a needle into a vein of its leg. Tranquilizers cause dogs to become very much less responsive to other stimuli. The final act of injecting the lethal solution will cause less reaction in the tranquilized animal.

When the lethal solution is injected into the vein, the dog will be dead almost immediately. The dog may take a few gasping breaths, but it will be completely unconscious as soon as the lethal drug enters its circulatory system. Occasionally a dog will vocalize, urinate, or defecate while it succumbs. These spasms are not an indication of pain or distress; they are reflex actions of the dog's nervous system shutting down.

Should I be there when my dog is euthanized?

That depends entirely on your preference; do what will disturb you the least. If you will feel better observing that your dog did not suffer, stay with it while it is euthanized. If you want to avoid watching, leave the dog and wait somewhere else. Go home if you'd rather not be there at all. Ask a friend to take your dog to the clinic for euthanasia if you can't bear the thought of taking it yourself. Personally we feel that the least disturbing procedure is for the veterinarian to give the dog a tranquilizer and have the owner stay with the dog until it is asleep or nearly asleep, then for the veterinarian to take the dog into another room for the actual euthanasia.

Don't be ashamed to shed tears when you must have your dog euthanized. And don't be surprised if the veterinarian or the clinic staff shed tears with you. This is a situation that nobody ever gets used to.

What do I do with the remains?

When deciding what to do with your dog's remains, do

whatever is the least disturbing to you. There are several options:

> Take the body home and bury it on your own property, with or without some sort of a casket. You can ask someone to dig a grave for you, you can dig it yourself, or you can hire the neighbor's husky child to do the digging. Very few municipalities have rules forbidding the burial of small animals on private property, but you should first check.

> Have the veterinarian dispose of the body for you. Veterinarians usually employ a service that buries or cremates remains. In most cases, the services conduct mass burials or mass cremations. You can request an individual cremation and the return of the ashes; this service can be quite costly.

> Have the body buried in a pet cemetery. Each cemetery has its own rules and procedures involving caskets, headstones, and services. Pet cemeteries also can be quite costly.

Chapter 15
What Happens to My Dog if I Die?

What will happen to my dog if it outlives me? What happens to my dog if I become incapacitated? This is a very reasonable question for a senior citizen to ask. Even people who are not seniors should give this subject some thought. We never know what might happen and we should all be prepared for the unexpected.

We all want our dogs to have a comfortable life and good care, even if we are no longer able to provide for them. There are whole books written about this problem. Laws differ in each state. The general procedure is to set up a legal trust for your dog's care, deposit money in the trust account, appoint a guardian to care for the dog, and appoint a trustee to disperse the money for the remainder of the dog's life. These legal actions require you to consult (and pay) an attorney. Do you need to do all this? Probably not. Let's see how to keep it simple.

Be sure to do something. You can ignore the problem on the supposition that it won't happen, and if it does happen, you won't know anything about it anyway. If you do that, you are shirking your responsibility as an owner.

Be prepared. Always tell your next of kin and your attorney which individual or society is to be called to take custody of your dog in the event of your illness or death. Put it in writing. Include it in your will.

Is there someone who can give your dog a home?

Is there a person that would accept your dog into her family? If so, your problem is solved. Talk it over with her, just to be sure, and then make an entry in your will, "Susan is to get Rover and all his equipment."

If Susan is the person you hope she is, you don't have to tell her how to take care of the dog; she'll do what is best for him. If you wish, it's easy to will Susan a sum of money or property to accompany Rover. If Susan wouldn't welcome Rover without the money, she is not the person you are looking for.

BUDDY

I recently had a conversation with a 95-year-old relative who has a three-year-old Welsh terrier that she loves beyond reason. She said, "If something happens to me, I'm going to have in my will that Buddy gets put to sleep."

I was horrified, and I told her so. "How could you do that, to a perfectly healthy dog?" I asked.

"I'm afraid that someone would abuse him," she replied. "It's better that he goes to sleep than take the chance."

Granted, Buddy is a handful, since his senior owner isn't much of a disciplinarian. Still, there are many people who like "active" dogs. Certainly, I told her, a home could be found for hers.

My elderly relative finally relented. "Well, you have to take him, then." I agreed. I hope she lives a long, long time.

If you don't have a "Susan," do you have a close friend or

relative that you can designate to assume temporary responsibility for Rover's future but that doesn't want to or isn't able to provide a permanent home for your dog? The duty of this person would be to seek a suitable new owner for Rover and to maintain the dog, perhaps in a boarding kennel on a limited time basis, until an owner can be found. It would be appropriate to will this person a small sum of money for board until your dog can be placed in a new home.

If Rover is a purebred dog, perhaps you can find a breed rescue group who will assume responsibility for him if you no longer can. Rescue groups try to place dogs of their specific breed. They often maintain individual dogs in the members' own homes until another owner is found.

Breed rescue groups can be a good source of new homes; knowledgeable individuals who are interested in the breed frequently investigate the groups' Web sites to look for adoptable dogs. When you find an appropriate rescue group, call its chairman and discuss the process of leaving Rover in its care if it ever becomes necessary. It would be appropriate to include a monetary donation to the group to help defray the cost of Rover's care.

Locate a breed rescue group on the Internet by indicating the breed and clicking on "search." There will be many entries for each breed, including several for rescue groups. Pick the one closest to your locality. If you are not computer literate, ask your grandchild to do it for you.

Many areas have organizations of people who wish to find homes for pets of all breeds and mixed breeds, but that do not have shelters of their own. Contacting these groups might be a good idea if Rover is not a purebred dog. Again, discuss how to leave Rover in the group's care if it is ever necessary. These organizations may be hard to locate, since they have no central site and are seldom listed under "pets" or "kennels" in the telephone book. Your local veterinary office is the best place to ask.

A no-kill animal shelter is a possible alternative.

If you have no friends or relatives to call upon to determine Rover's future, consider a private Humane Society shelter in your area. Note, this is not the dog warden. The local dog warden must accept any and all dogs that are found or relinquished in the area. The warden keeps these dogs for a specified number of days, and if they are not claimed or purchased, the warden euthanizes the dogs. This is not the fate you want for Rover, but it is the fate of many dogs whose senior owners make no provisions for their future. Someone dies and the next-of-kin doesn't know what to do with his dog so they dump it at the "pound."

The "No-Kill" movement in Humane Societies began some 20 years ago and has spread to include the majority of private shelters in the United States. Simply stated, No-Kill humane society shelters are committed to find homes for almost every animal in their care. This includes old animals and many animals with physical or behavioral problems. No-Kill shelters do not euthanize an animal unless the animal has an overwhelming problem that would prevent it from re-entering society. No-Kill shelters employ veterinarians and animal trainers to try to rectify whatever health and behavior issues their resident animals might have, and to return as many animals as possible to pet homes.

A Humane Society animal shelter is quite different from a city or county dog "pound." Humane Societies are not a part of local, city, or state government, although some of these organizations may have contracts with government to care for some of the unwanted animals in the locality. Humane Society shelters are privately financed, privately staffed, and their board of directors privately determines their policies.

The "No-Kill" movement in animal shelters began some 20 years ago and has spread to include the majority of Humane Society shelters in the United States. A No-Kill shelter never euthanizes an animal just because it is old. A No-Kill shelter never euthanizes an animal because it needs surgery or medical treatment to restore it to health. The only animals that are put to death at a No-Kill shelter are those that are beyond medical help and those that are so vicious as to be a danger to the community.

Many Humane Society shelters also neuter or spay every animal before it leaves the premises. They do this to help prevent the births of surplus dogs and cats and to eliminate the problems of un-altered animals.

How can I find the right shelter? How can I be sure that the shelter will do the best thing for my dog?

Look in the yellow pages of the telephone book under "animal shelters." Be sure you haven't selected a dog warden, who is likely to be listed under city or county kennels. Pick out the nearest Humane Society shelter and phone them to determine their open hours. Go take a look at the place.

Depending on the organization's budget, the shelter may be elaborate or simple, but is should be clean and relatively odor-free. Consider that if it became necessary, would you be happy having Rover spend any time at this shelter? Talk to the personnel at the front desk. Are they courteous and helpful?

Take a look at the areas that contain dogs waiting for adoption. Are the cages clean? Do the dogs have ample room? Do they have water? Do they have toys and appropriate beds?

If you find the shelter to be acceptable, ask to speak with the shelter manager or the humane officer. State your business. You want to determine the best outcome for your pet in the event of your demise or incapacitation. Shelter workers are busy people; you may have to make an appointment and come back at another time.

When you get an opportunity to speak to the shelter manager or the humane officer, question them about the shelter's policy on dog placement and euthanasia. Don't just ask "Are you a No-Kill shelter?" Nearly everyone will tell you that yes, they are. Let them tell you about the shelter's euthanasia policy. Many shelters will have one or more handouts explaining their procedures.

If you are satisfied with the shelter and the people who run it, explain to the manager or the humane officer that your aim is to locate the best place to find your dog a new home if you predecease it. They will understand; they have probably heard the statement dozens of times.

Take your new knowledge and all the brochures they provided home with you and think it over. You might even elect to become a member of the Humane Society yourself. If you decide that the shelter will be the best place for Rover, consider if you want to leave the shelter some money in your will to accompany your dog. This donation should be over and above any contributions you choose to make during your life. Remember, private contributions, fund raising events, and adoption fees fund all the work of Humane Societies. No Humane Society ever has enough money to help every needy animal.

Whatever money you will to the Society will have only one

effect on the treatment that Rover will receives there: the personnel will have a greater appreciation of the love you felt for your canine companion and your effort to insure it good care after your death. Peace of mind comes with advanced planning. We all hope that none of this planning will be necessary, but don't you feel better once you have insured your dog's future?

Part V: Getting a New Dog

Chapter 16
The Pros and Cons of a New Dog

"Dad, I'm so sorry about Rover. Let's go get you another dog right away, one as much like Rover as possible."

"I told you to get rid of that dog long ago. Now you won't have fur on the carpet and can travel any time you want."

"You don't need another dog." At your age, it's all you can do to take care of yourself. You spent too much money on it anyway."

Everyone offers advice. Your children, your friends, your neighbors, even casual acquaintances will let you know what they think. Unfortunately, some of the well-meant advice will be against getting another dog. To whom should you listen?

Listen only to yourself. Unless you live with someone who shares the care of your dog, you have the one and only vote. If someone in your household helps with the dog's care, that person should be involved in the decision, but yours is the deciding opinion. After all, it's your companion.

Don't make your decision too quickly. Wait a few weeks to see if you like life better without a dog. Wait at least a week, especially if you're not sure you want another dog. It's not hard to find another great canine companion, but it is heartbreaking to give one up if you change your mind.

What should I consider in making my decision?

Ask yourself the following questions:

> How much do I miss having a dog? Do I hate to come home to an empty house? Do I automatically reach for a furry head to pat? Was I less lonely when Rover was here? Do I find myself talking to myself because there is nobody else to talk to?

> Was I more active when I had a dog? Was a dog important to my health and physical well being? Did I get more exercise walking and taking care of a dog? Does my doctor recommend that I keep up physical activity such as walking, even without my dog?

> Am I uneasy without my watchdog? Do I worry when I hear footsteps outside? Do I check my doors several times, even though I know I locked them? Do I hate to go anywhere in the car without my dog for protection and company?

> Do I feel relief that I don't have to care for a dog? Is it nice to sleep later in the morning and not have to get up because Rover needs to go outside? Is it better not to have to go out in bad weather with Rover? Do I enjoy not having to come home to care for my dog?

> Is my house and yard cleaner? Do I care about that? Did I really mind the hair on my clothes and carpeting? Would I rather not have to clean up the yard?

> Am I relieved that I no longer have the expense of dog care? Do I appreciate the saving, now that I don't have to buy dog food and pay veterinary bills? Is it a relief not to worry about the dog's health? Can I save money on my rental home now that I don't have to make a deposit to cover the damage a dog might cause? Can I now live where dogs are not permitted?

> Am I tired of listening to advice? Do my family and friends tell me that I'm too old for another dog? That a dog is too much trouble and expense? That now I can travel and visit them? Should I silence these people by taking their advice? Will I hear endless criticism if I do get another dog, and is the dog's companionship worth it? Should I be impolite and tell people that my decision is none of their business?

Could I enjoy someone else's dog?

It won't be the same as having your own, but would you be happy to borrow the neighbor's dog to take walking? Should you volunteer at a shelter and help care for and walk the homeless dogs there? Your efforts will be greatly appreciated by the shelter staff, and anticipated by the canine population.

How about a cat?

Some people love dogs but never would consider owning a cat. These individuals never had the opportunity to listen to a good purr, to feel a furry body on their lap, to be met at the door by a happy little animal. A cat can be nearly the same companionship as a dog, but without some of the drawbacks.

> Cats don't have to be walked on a leash in all kinds of weather.

> Cats can stay alone for a couple of days if necessary, if food and litter are provided for them.

> Cats don't need obedience training. Cats don't chew table legs. Cats don't bark and annoy the neighbors. Cats (usually) don't mess on the rug if appropriate litter is provided for them.

> Cats are easier and less expensive to feed than are large

dogs, even though those little cans of cat food are rather expensive.

Should I consider a pet bird?

Birds can be a lot of fun. Granted, they are not the companions that are dogs and cats, but birds are other living things that you can care for and enjoy. A pet bird is even less trouble than a cat, and causes less mess in the house unless you count a few seeds on the floor. Purchasing a bird, cage, and supplies will be less expensive (unless you chose one of the large parrots) than purchasing a dog or a cat and having it vaccinated, spayed, or neutered.

The birds most commonly kept as pets include canaries, parakeets, and some of the other species of psitticines (parrots). Canaries are pretty, male canaries sing nicely and are entertaining, but canaries are seldom very tame. Unless you are content just to look at your pet, there are other birds that make more interactive companions.

Parakeets are the least expensive and most common pet birds. A parakeet that is tamed when it is young will sit on your finger or shoulder. Parakeets can be trained to talk a little. They exist well in small cages and eat inexpensive food.

Larger parrots such as cockatoos and macaws are known for their taking ability. Large birds that are tame are really amusing pets. But cockatoos, macaws, and parrots have some important drawbacks:

> These birds, their cages, and their feed can be very expensive.

> Most of these birds can be annoying screamers.

> Without daily cleaning, these birds can produce large

amounts of debris and scatter it about the house. If you decide on a large parrot, you better get a new vacuum cleaner to pick up the feathers and seeds.

A cockatiel may be your best choice for a pet bird. Cockatiels and cages suitable for them are relatively inexpensive. Hand-tamed cockatiels are often available, although a little more costly than untamed ones. Cockatiels come in several pretty colors, are easy to care for, and can be provided with seed and water and left alone for a day or two. Cockatiels are affectionate; their natural call is cheerful and entertaining.

Chapter 17
Choosing a New Dog

Yes, you were much happier when you had a dog. You had a warning if someone came to the house. You had a companion to go on walks with you. Most important, you were not alone. You decided you want another dog.

Should I get a dog just like the last one?

Don't try to get another Rover or another Princie. Even if you get a dog of the identical breed, color, and sex as your last one, it won't be the same dog. Start over; look for the dog that will best fit into your life.

There must have been some things you would have changed about Rover. Did you ever wish that he were smaller? Bigger? Had less hair to groom or to sweep up? Now is your chance to get a dog with all the characteristics you prefer.

Make a mental list. Make a written list if there are many items to consider. Even with a list, you'll have to work hard not to submit to impulse when you meet some of the dogs that need new homes. "But he has such a cute face" is not really the best way to choose a new companion, even though I've done it myself.

What should I look for in my new dog?

Chose a dog of the right size for your life. Only you can be the judge of the best size dog for you. Large dogs tend to want more exercise than smaller dogs, and of course, large dogs need more food.

Are you willing and able to brush out your long-haired dog's dead hair? Are you comfortable with taking your dog to a groomer (and paying for it) to have a bath and a haircut? Keep in mind that all dogs shed. Short-haired dogs shed short hairs, long-haired dogs shed long hairs. The so-called "no-shed" breeds such as poodles also shed. You don't see poodle hair on the floor because the loose dead hair stays matted in the dog's coat and must be removed by clipping, brushing, and combing. If caring for your dog's coat is a problem, consider getting a low-maintenance dog. A short-haired dog might be best.

You know what you like. Nobody should tell you to get a Chihuahua if you are a Springer Spaniel fancier. Just use your head and don't select a breed or a crossbred that is known for traits that may be difficult for you to deal with. Don't select a collie if you'd rather not comb and brush out dog hair. Don't select a beagle if your neighbors don't like the noise.

Don't get a puppy. The first six to nine months of a dog's life is nothing but work. A very young dog needs the most attention, the most training, the most discipline, and the most money spent on vaccines and neutering. A puppy will need to be housebroken and cleaned up after. A puppy will probably make it necessary to replace some shoes and rugs. Save yourself time, effort, money, and aggravation. If you get an adult dog, you can see exactly what you are getting instead of possibly being disappointed in a few months.

You will find a far greater selection of adult dogs that need homes than you will find puppies. Take your time and select from the literally dozens of great prospects.

Don't get an old, old dog. Very old dogs, like very old people, can develop health problems that could become troublesome and expensive for you to care for. Even though some shelter workers try to convince senior citizens that older dogs are for them, ordinarily it is best to reject a dog that is more than seven or eight years old. Remember that larger breeds usually have shorter lives than smaller breeds. An eight-year-old Great Dane is definitely a senior, but an eight-year-old fox terrier is just middle-aged.

One of the joys of getting an adult dog is that it probably housebroken. It is probably leash-trained. It is not likely to chew everything in sight. This doesn't mean that you should just pretend that it has lived all its life in your house, but it does mean that it will be easy to acclimate to your routine and to your environment.

If possible, ask why your prospective new dog is in need of another home. Some dogs will be relinquished because of a death in the family, relocation, or even a family addition such as a new baby. A dog that was a stray will have no history, but that doesn't mean that a stray can't be a wonderful pet. Once it was someone's pet; now it could be yours.

Where should I get my new dog?

Start your search at one of the many organizations that place dogs in new homes. There will be several in or near your location. Not all of these organizations are the same, so be sure to ask plenty of questions.

Municipal or county dog warden.

City, county, or municipal dog kennels are operated by a dog warden who is a public servant and is required to obey local ordinances. Dog wardens impound strays and must accept any dog that is relinquished by its owner. In most instances, the dogs at the warden's kennel are offered for sale for a predetermined number of days and are euthanized when their time runs out.

Public facilities handle strays and relinquished dogs in many different ways. Some facilities give their inmates no medical care, no vaccinations, and no evaluation of the dog's temperament. Some facilities vaccinate only dogs that are considered to be more likely to be purchased. Some facilities have a working arrangement to send friendly, healthy dogs to other placement groups instead of euthanizing them.

If you look for your new dog at a dog warden's, you must be aware that you are taking a chance of getting an animal that may have health or behavior problems. You will probably have to have the dog spayed or neutered, vaccinated, and treated for parasites. On the plus side, if you buy a dog at a local or county facility, you probably will be saving its life.

Private humane society shelters.

Donations and fund-raisers support private humane societies, not government funds. These organizations are not required to accept any and all dogs that are offered to them, although most private shelters attempt to take as many animals in need of help as they possibly can.

Humane societies are dedicated to reducing the population of unwanted pet animals. The national trend in private humane society shelters is to place only animals that have been surgically sterilized. If you buy a dog from a private shelter, you'll probably get one that has already been spayed or neutered.

At most private humane societies, every dog is vaccinated against the most important canine diseases. Every dog is checked for internal and external parasites and treated if necessary. A trainer may evaluate the dog's disposition and establish recommendations for placement in a new home. If you get a dog from a private humane society, you'll know its health status, its vaccination status, and quite a bit about its training and behavior.

If you buy a dog from a private humane society, it will cost more than a dog from a "dog pound," since a portion of the cost of the surgery, the vaccinations, and the other treatment will be included in the purchase price. Still, you will get an unbelievable bargain, since everything the dog needs at the time will have been already done—and paid for.

Ask your veterinarian.

Veterinarians often are notified when one of their clients' animals needs a new home. The veterinarian who has vaccinated, spayed, neutered, and treated a dog will be well aware of the dog's temperament and health. His or her recommendation will be valid. You don't have to ask the veterinarian personally; the secretary will know about any dogs that are available.

Other private placement groups.

Private placement groups exist in many localities. These groups consist of concerned people who want to help. Many of these groups don't have shelters; they foster dogs in their own homes or even pay to have the dogs kept in boarding kennels until they can find permanent homes for them.

Find these placement groups by asking your veterinarian (or

the secretary) if there are any in your area. Ask if the groups are reliable; it is not unheard of for a very few of these groups to misrepresent the dogs they want to place, in hopes of getting the dogs into new homes.

Breed rescue groups on the Internet.

If you are interested in getting a specific breed of dog, you can locate a private placement group for that breed on the Internet. Ask any search engine for "collie rescue" for example. You'll get several sites. Pick the one closest to you. They'll probably have a list (and sometimes photographs) of the dogs they have available for adoption. If one sounds like it should be your new dog, ask for details with an e-mail. If you aren't computer-literate, ask your grandchildren to help. They'll know how to do it.

Breed rescue groups usually screen their applicants and usually place only dogs that have been spayed or neutered. There will be a charge covering the care and medical treatment for each dog; again, this will be a great bargain over having to pay for the treatment yourself.

Dog breeders.

Breeders of purebred dogs are not only sources of puppies. Often a breeder has an adult dog that needs a new home, either because its reproductive life is over, or because someone who purchased it as a puppy has returned it to the breeder.

Adult dogs are in less demand than are puppies. There is likely to be a charge for a purebred adult dog, but it should be significantly less than the cost of a puppy of the same breed. Most breeders will have their adult dogs spayed or neutered before placement, which is a justifiable reason for charging a reasonable amount for the dog.

If the breeder has nothing suitable to offer, perhaps she can refer you to someone in her kennel club who does. It's always worth a try.

Advertisement in newspapers.

"Free to good home." You'll see this in the pet classified advertisements. Newspapers frequently carry advertisements for adult dogs for sale as well as free. These ads might be a wonderful source for a new dog, but be careful. Question the present owner to find out exactly why the dog is being offered. If you have any doubts that the dog has an unacceptable problem, don't even go to look at it. You are more likely to get dependable information about a dog from sources other than newspaper advertisements.

What will my new dog cost?

Your new dog may be absolutely free. But it could cost you several hundred dollars. The price of a dog is so variable that there is no way to make a valid estimate without knowing all the facts.

You want an adult animal, not a puppy. You want a pet, not a breeding animal, not a show dog, not a hunting dog. If you are compassionate and lucky, you'll be getting a dog that is in need of a new home, from a source that is in need of finding that home.

The cost of an adult dog from a private party is whatever the seller thinks he can get. Some people feel that if a buyer pays at least something for a dog, the dog will be more valued than if it were free. Before you buy a new dog, consider what you are getting for your money:

> Is it spayed or neutered?
> Has it had its vaccines and is it free of parasites?
> Is the dog's type and temperament right for you?
> Has the dog had the training to fit into your life?

If you answer, "yes" to all these questions, the dog is a bargain, no matter what the price.

How can I get my new dog to adjust to my lifestyle?

Set up the Safe Place for the new dog before you bring the dog home. Make the dog feel comfortable there with a blanket, a bowl of water, and a few toys. For the first week or two that you own the new dog, don't leave it loose in the house when you are not supervising it. Very soon you will know when the dog is trustworthy in your home.

Decide where the "bathroom" will be ahead of time. Your new adult dog will probably be housebroken, but it still needs to have the correct habits established in a new place. Plan regular feeding and walking times. Take the new dog to the "bathroom" location often.

Try to feed your new dog the same food that it has been eating. Avoid diarrhea and other intestinal problems. Change its diet gradually to the food you prefer.

Interact with your new dog as frequently as you can. Pet it, play with it, feed it, and take it for walks. Return the dog to its Safe Place when you are otherwise occupied. Soon your new dog will be your very best friend.

Appendix

Advisory and financial assistance.

Local agencies are the groups that offer assistance to dog owners. Many of these organizations confine their activities to residents of one county or one area, although some agencies serve everyone who needs their help. Call your veterinarian or the nearest humane society for information:

> Spay-neuter clinics; low-cost spay-neuter certificates
> Rabies clinics
> Vaccination clinics
> Mobile veterinarians who will come to you
> Rescue group for a certain breed of dog
> Getting a new dog or finding a new home for a dog

Humane societies and veterinarians will know where and when these services are offered, what the services cost, and who is eligible to receive the services. Humane societies and rescue groups often provide certificates for these services at no cost or reduced cost to seniors. All the telephone numbers you need are in your local telephone book.

Other Services.

Find providers of other services in your local telephone book. Look in the Yellow Pages under "kennels" or under "pet."

> Dog Walker or pet sitting services
> Boarding and grooming kennels
> Dog trainers or dog training classes

Assistance dogs.

To find a dog trained especially to help those with handicaps, ask your health professional for a referral. Dogs that lead the blind, dogs that alert the hearing-impaired, dogs that offer assistance to people with limited mobility, all are available from national organizations. Your doctor, your nurse, or your health aid will have the information you need.

Professional assistance dog training organizations are supported largely by private donations. Recipients of the dogs are asked to pay only part of the cost. Each recipient and his or her dog must undergo a training period to insure that the dog and new owner will work together.

A few trainers offer assistance dogs for sale, but are not connected to any national dog training organization. These trainers operate for-profit businesses. If one of these trainers is recommended to you, ask for evidence that his or her dogs are properly trained to perform their tasks. Be especially careful if the assistance dog is offered for sale at a very much larger price than those offered by the national organizations.

Where to buy supplies and equipment.

Collars of all types, leashes, chains, tie-out cables, and most of the other items that are described and recommended are often available in nearby retail stores in the following sections:

> The pet food isle of your local grocery store will have some of the more commonly used items.

> Pet stores, especially the large national chain stores such as PetSmart carry most of the items you need.

> Local feed or farm stores and hardware stores usually sell dog equipment. These stores will be a good source of fencing, kennel fence panels, and kennels for Safe Places. National chain stores will have a larger selection of equipment and often lower prices than will smaller local businesses.

> Super stores such as Wal-Mart and K-Mart have large pet departments and are good sources of dog equipment and supplies.

Invisible Fence, other brands of electronic fence, wooden fencing, and wire fencing all will be listed in your local Yellow Pages under "Fence."

Mail order supply companies.

These are three of the largest mail-order dog supply companies in the US. You can locate many other companies on the Internet. Write, email, or call toll-free for their printed catalogs.

Foster and Smith Pet Supply
P. O. Box 100
Rhinelander, WI 54501

1-800-381-7179
www.drsfostersmith.com

JB Wholesale Pet Supplies, Inc.
5 Raritan Road
Oakland, NJ 07436
1-800-872-6027
www.jbpet.com

Jeffers Pet
P. O. Box 100
Dothan, aL 36302
1-800-533-3377
www.jefferspet.com

Innotek bark collars and fences, etc.
Invisible Technologies, Inc.
Garrett, Indiana
1-800-826-5527
www.innotek.net

Tri-tronics® bark collars and fences, etc.
P. O. Box 17660
Tucson, aZ 85731
1-800-456-4343
www.tritronics.com

Citronella collars.

Many brands are available locally, in catalogs, and on the Internet. Search "citronella bark-control collars."

Identification tags can be ordered from many sources. Humane societies, pet shops, and hardware stores often have forms that you can fill out and mail.

Buying on the Internet.

If you don't use the Internet, go to any public library and ask the librarian in the technology division for help. He or she will be happy to find the appropriate site for you. Or ask a grandchild to help. Most children are very computer-knowledgeable these days.

Select from the online catalog or ask for a catalog to be mailed to you so that you can choose the products you need at your leisure. These are some of the search terms to use:

> Dog supplies
> Pet supplies
> Bark collars
> Identification tags
> Electronic fences

The cost of electronic equipment such as bark collars and other items often is significantly lower when ordered on the Internet. The competition is keen and many suppliers offer sales. Before you buy, search for the item and compare the prices. Buy Specialty items by mail such as Innotek bark-control collars, zone barriers, fences, etc.

Index

Printed in the United States
142475LV00002B/42/P